Sixth Edition

PUBLIC SECTOR ACCOUNTING

Rowan Jones

Birmingham Business School
Birmingham University

Maurice Pendlebury

Cardiff Business School
Cardiff University

**Financial Times
Prentice Hall**
is an imprint of

Harlow, England • London • New York • Boston • San Francisco • Toronto • Sydney • Singapore • Hong Kong
Tokyo • Seoul • Taipei • New Delhi • Cape Town • Madrid • Mexico City • Amsterdam • Munich • Paris • Milan

Pearson Education Limited
Edinburgh Gate
Harlow
Essex CM20 2JE
England

and Associated Companies throughout the world

Visit us on the World Wide Web at:
www.pearsoned.co.uk

First published under the Pitman imprint in Great Britain in 1984
Second edition published 1988
Third edition published 1992
Fourth edition published 1996
Fifth edition published 2000
Sixth edition published 2010

ISBN: 978-0-273-72036-2

British Library Cataloguing-in-Publication Data
A catalogue record for this book is available from the British Library

Library of Congress Cataloging-in-Publication Data
A catalog record for this book is available from the Library of Congress

10 9 8 7 6 5 4 3 2 1
13 12 11 10

Typeset in 9.5/12.5pt Stone Serif by 35
Printed and bound in Great Britain by Ashford Colour Press Ltd, Gosport, Hampshire

The publisher's policy is to use paper manufactured from sustainable forests.

Contents

Preface

This book is about government budgeting, accounting and auditing, from an accountant's perspective. Government budgeting, particularly, can underemphasise – even ignore – accounting. Our purpose is to portray the whole of government, being the core part of the public sector, through the eyes of accountants. We do this by concentrating on the possibilities of accounting technique. Throughout, we combine discussion of the importance of the techniques with their limitations. Nevertheless, the book depends on the importance of accounting technique.

Historically and around the world, introductory accounting and intermediate accounting are taught in the context of for-profit organisations. This book assumes a basic understanding of such accounting. Its method is to focus on those matters that can be different in governments, even while there is significant overlap in accounting for governments, non-profits and for-profits.

Chapter 1 provides an introduction to the nature of the public sector, the heart of which is the sovereignty of governments ultimately controlled by politicians. It introduces the nature of government, governance and public management, public finance, public money and the role of accountants in the public sector.

Chapter 2 is an overview of performance measurement, which permeates all aspects of government budgeting, accounting and auditing. It identifies distinctive challenges of performance measurement for accounting.

Chapter 3 details the technical fundamentals of accounting. These are the same in all organisations, whether governmental, for-profit or not-for-profit, but the public sector context shifts the emphasis among these fundamentals. The chapter also discusses two other forms of accounting – national accounting and government budgeting – that complement and sometimes compete with public sector accounting.

Chapters 4, 5 and 6 are concerned with budgeting. Chapter 4 deals broadly with budgetary policies and processes. Chapter 5 explains the common forms, and associated content, that government budgets can take. Chapter 6 concerns budgetary control, which is a dominant function of accounting, but one that can be exercised in different ways.

Chapter 7 addresses costing techniques, which by their nature are less extensively used in government than in for-profits but, when they are used, can have important consequences for managers, politicians, service recipients and taxpayers.

Chapter 8 is about financial reporting. There are significant overlaps between reporting standards for all organisations, but there are distinctive issues for governments – budgetary reporting, consolidated financial statements and special accrual accounting issues. There are also particular issues relating to policymaking and policymakers' conceptual frameworks.

Chapter 9 deals with auditing. Here, too, there is much overlap between organisations of all kinds, but the distinctive issues in government are of importance. These are the definition of audit independence; financial, regularity and performance audits; internal audits and internal control; attitudes to materiality; and budget auditing.

Every chapter includes a further reading list. These are not usually developments of technical accounting matters. Some of the publications listed are from non-accounting literature, for the accountant to use in a wider understanding of technique. Most, however, are from accounting literature. This typically takes the understanding of technique as given but then situates it in wider contexts, allowing a fuller discussion of the strengths and weaknesses of technique. This is especially necessary given that technical accounting developments tend to be made by accounting's standard-setting bodies or consultants, not academics. Nevertheless, it remains true that accounting technique and this wider context are difficult to marry. There is little theoretical understanding of the relationship between government accounting systems and social, economic and political success. The further reading lists therefore mainly provide a basis for developing our understanding.

The illustrative examples used throughout are generic, for the mythical City of Eutopia, and themselves are based on pure matters of accounting technique. In Eutopia's financial statements we use generic forms rather than arbitrarily imposing one particular set of accounting standards. The examples use numbers but not mainly for the purposes of training the reader in making calculations. Rather, this is done to make the illustrations more meaningful. We represent Eutopia not as an ideal government but an ideal for understanding the possibilities and limits of government accounting technique. We willingly concede that soldiers, police officers, social workers, teachers and nurses (among others) might imagine that Eutopia is situated on the edges of an infernal place to which its accountants daily commute.

This sixth edition is very different from the previous editions. The earlier editions were essentially the first edition, published in 1982, with marginal changes made since then. The sixth edition, however, reflects the fact that there have been fundamental changes in public sector accounting over this last generation and a half – changes that no doubt, in part, have been facilitated by the information revolution we are living through. The major changes since the 1970s are that there were then no sets of public sector accounting standards, but now there are, including one international set, and some of them are based on for-profit standards. The only set of public sector auditing standards then was that used by the US Federal Government, known (as it still is) as the Yellow Book. It was, however, actually a booklet of 54 small pages. Also, the recording, use and publication of output measures were then the exception, but now they are ubiquitous. The result of all these changes is that there has been a narrowing of the differences between government, non-profit and for-profit accounting.

The changes have also brought greater comparative understanding of government accounting between jurisdictions within each country and between countries. No longer is it possible to make the joke, as one professor did in 1986 when introducing a seminar on 'international government accounting', that the term seemed to him to be an oxymoron. Having said that, Anglophone accounting still dominates the discourse (if quantity of literature is the measure), which is an especially troubling matter given that, presumably, most government accounting in the world is not practised in English. This book does not help in this: it is firmly Anglophone, primarily as a generalisation of UK and some US theory and practice.

Rowan Jones and Maurice Pendlebury

Acknowledgements

The authors acknowledge, with the usual caveat exempting them from blame, the following, who have personally helped over the years in our understanding of public sector accounting: in the USA, Gary Giroux and James Patton; in Europe, within the Comparative International Governmental Accounting Research network (CIGAR), Klaus Lüder and Aad Bac, and Berit Adam, Eugenio Caperchione, Jan van Helden, Susana Jorge, Evelyne Lande, Frode Mellemvik, Norvald Monsen, Vicente Montesinos, Riccardo Mussari, Salme Näsi, Kuno Schedler, Jean-Claude Scheid and Torbjörn Tagesson.

Chapter 1

The nature of the public sector

Most of the accounting discipline is taught and learnt in the context of businesses. The heart of the public sector is the sovereignty of governments ultimately controlled by politicians. This provides a very different context for public sector as opposed to private sector accounting.

1.1 The nature of government

The heart of the public sector is the sovereignty of governments ultimately controlled by politicians. For a national government, this sovereignty extends over a whole country, including its economy; for a state government within a federation, the sovereignty extends over its individual state. There is also, in the European Union, the sovereignty of the Union itself, being of supranational government.

At all levels of government, this sovereignty has different elements of governance. In principle, it is ultimately embodied in one person, generically called the 'head of state' ('king/queen', 'president'), and then exercised by a legislature making laws ('parliament', 'congress'); an executive carries out and enforces those laws (headed by a 'prime minister', 'president', 'governor') and a judiciary interpreting them in the courts. Ultimate power and responsibility in the legislatures and executive (and, in republics, in heads of state) are held by politicians. Legislatures are also supported by a typically small staff, while the executive is typically supported by a large staff of political appointees and career civil servants.

The sovereign governments have, below them, local governments, which do not make law and do not therefore have legislatures or judiciaries. In local governments, however, power and responsibility are also ultimately held by politicians, supported by paid staff ('civil servants', 'public servants', 'officers', 'managers'). There are varying senses, depending on the particular local area, in which each local government is below the sovereign government. Local governments are dependent, and often almost entirely dependent on higher-level governments, including for money, though there are a few major exceptions in which a very large city may be significantly free of control by any higher-level government.

From a financial point of view, the distinctive feature of sovereign and many local governments is their power to tax. If a local government does not have the power directly, it will receive the product of taxes from a higher-level government in some form of government grant. Taxation is used to redistribute income and provide other economic incentives but its primary purpose is to pay for governing: at national level, for its relations with supranational governments and the rest of the world; for the regulation of industries, particularly banks, financial markets and the utilities; and for the services of the justice system, the central bank, defence, education, health, police, social services, transport. In the definitive form, these services – financed at bottom by taxation – are provided to the service recipients free at the point of delivery. These are the senses in which they are known as 'public services', though there are many practical cases in which the link of a particular public service to taxation is not direct and in which some form of payment has to be made by service recipients.

While it is useful, even necessary in general discourse, to use the term 'a government' as though referring to a single organisation, a government at any level is typically a complex set of organisations, having complex relationships with other organisations within the country and beyond. Governments are made up of legislature, executive, judiciary, but also departments, agencies; they often own or, particularly using their power to provide money, control for-profit entities ('public corporations', 'nationalised industries', 'state-owned enterprises', though these might have break-even or loss-making targets) and non-profit entities ('not-for-profit', 'charities', 'quasi-autonomous non-governmental organisations (quangos)', 'public bodies'); they are in formal partnership with non-profit and for-profit entities, sometimes as the major partner, sometimes minor; and they award contracts to, and otherwise buy from (known as procurement), for-profit and non-profit entities.

A common way of trying to make sense of the complex webs of relationships that make up modern countries is to distinguish between private interests and the public interest. At one extreme, we would identify each individual as having his or her inalienable, private rights; the private interests might come together in groups (families, owner-managed companies, partnerships, public companies) and we would refer to them as being in the private sector. At the other extreme, we would identify the inalienable, sovereign right of a national government to protect the public interest, and refer to the sovereign government as being in the public sector.

Even though the above is a helpful distinction in modern countries, assigning every other organisation to one of the two sectors is not straightforward. One way of trying to make it clearer is to put some organisations into a 'third sector' made up of non-profits, which provide services to service recipients free at the point of delivery (and, hence, are 'public', deserving relief from taxation), but are, at bottom, paid for by voluntary contributions (not taxation). This third sector is sometimes referred to as the 'voluntary sector'.

The fact is that different disciplines, reflecting different worldviews, define the public sector differently: politics, public administration/management, sociology, law and economics offer different, though sometimes overlapping, perspectives using a range of concepts, including ownership, control, taxation, accountability, entitlement and rights. If there is no agreement on what the public sector is, it is no surprise that there is disagreement about what it ought to be.

A core meaning of government is control, as difficult as that word can be to define succinctly. The extent to which a national government controls its economy, its own organisation and other lower-level governments, as well as the private organisations that help to deliver its services, is an important part of the nature of government, as is the degree of control that each other governmental organisation has over its own affairs. Control of an economy has, in modern governments, ranged from central control of all sectors (centrally planned economies) to minimal regulation and little control of the private sector.

The term 'public sector' was first used in 1952 by an economist who, having spent most of his life in Hungary (then part of the Soviet Union), when writing in the USA, offered comparisons of economic systems, synthesising them into three groups: countries like the USA that emphasised economic freedom; countries like the Soviet Union that had adopted central planning; and countries like the UK and France that had traditionally emphasised 'Western economic freedom' but in the previous two decades had shifted to more of a compromise between 'freedom' and 'planning'. In other words, the term was adopted to focus on the mix between the public and private sectors in an economy.

The mixed economies had significantly increased the role of government since the Depression of the 1930s and in response to major changes in society after World War II, even if there was a difference in degree between the USA and Europe. The obvious failures of the markets (periodic episodes of high unemployment being the most immediate, but also including widening gaps between the rich and the poor) provided clear motivations. Economics analyses these failures as resulting, for example, from incomplete markets and/or information failures, the failure of the individual costs and benefits of providing and receiving a particular good or service, which are captured in the market price, to capture the costs and benefits to everyone else (the externalities) and the fact that some goods and services ('public goods') will not be supplied by markets or, if they are, will be supplied in insufficient quantity (because individuals can enjoy them at no cost and it is difficult or impossible to exclude them from enjoying them, such as a lighthouse).

Control of an economy includes budgeting and accounting for that economy, and though there are strong parallels with control of a single governmental organisation, the two forms of control are different. For an economy, the mother disciplines (as it were) are economics and statistics, not accounting.

National government control over lower-level governments is a formal matter of law. Often that is constitutional, but it can also be economic and financial. For example, a federal government may have no legal right to control a state's local government, but may offer grants that specify how that money must be spent and accounted for, with concomitant auditing requirements. Similarly, a local government in a unitary state may legally be separate from the central government, but may have few finances of its own, being dependent on general grants from the centre that may not specify how they are to be spent but the overriding power of the purse provides the effective control.

The control that each governmental organisation has over its own affairs is where accounting has its most direct role, since accounting itself is primarily concerned with control. An important way of thinking about the degree of control, focusing on financial control, is to distinguish between a central financial control in each organisation (which may or may not be in the hands of accountants: particularly in a sovereign government, this may be in the hands of a ministry of finance, influenced by economists) and a devolved control. The emphasis in the first is a detailed control of means, while in the second the emphasis is on control of ends. Modern governments were established by having central control of the details of how money was spent, but this form of control now competes with, and has sometimes been supplanted by, a central control of the overall amount of money to be spent accompanied by a central control of what the spending achieves overall.

1.2 Governance and public management

Governance, here, is about the management of each government organisation and how that management is held accountable to those charged with governance within that organisation. In generic form, it focuses on the role of non-executive officers and the existence of an audit and assurance committee in relation to the management board of the organisation and with reporting lines for the internal auditors. It also focuses on delineating, in published form, the responsibilities of management separate from the responsibilities of the external auditors. The term 'governance' was originally a synonym for 'government' that had fallen from general usage. In recent decades, it re-emerged in the term 'corporate governance', in relation to the top management of public companies particularly. It came to be applied to all kinds of organisations. In government, it is not a way of thinking about government in its widest legal and political senses, but a way of thinking about each governmental organisation, such as a government department of a national government.

This emergence of the importance of the explicit responsibilities of governance coincided with an increase in the importance of internal control systems, in two ways. The systems have become more elaborate and more explicit. They have also, at least in principle, been extended to include all aspects of management and not just the long-standing financial aspects of internal control systems. Moreover, once internal control systems have been established, the emphasis is placed on management and those charged with governance managing the risks that the internal control system will break down.

The major impetus for strengthened systems of governance and internal control came from financial scandals, including financial reporting scandals. A significant marker in this was the establishment in 1985 in the USA of what is now the Committee of Sponsoring Organizations (COSO), a private sector body of five professional accounting associations, including the American Institute of Certified Public Accountants and the Institute of Internal Auditors, and the American Accounting Association, an academic accounting body. Its work on internal controls is palpable in the government auditing standards and requirements of the US Office of Management and Budget and the Government Accountability Office. The collapse of Enron in 2001, and associated business failures, added further impetus to its work. It is not yet clear what the implications of the banking crisis that began in 2007 will be for its work.

The public services that are provided to the service recipients free of charge are delivered by the military, teachers, doctors, nurses, police officers, social services officers, transport managers. Many of these service specialists are employed by governmental organisations, as military personnel and civil servants. These specialists are ultimately responsible to politicians and political appointees, but they also need to be managed. The public managers also have the responsibility of managing relationships with other governmental organisations and for-profit and non-profit organisations, the service specialists of which might better provide the public services under contract rather than as employees of the government. Public management includes specialist functions such as solicitors, human resource managers and financial managers. Also, the marketing function, while it was originally established to sell products and services for businesses, has an important role in the public sector, too. In many governmental organisations, the financial managers will mainly be accountants but, especially in sovereign governments, economists have important, perhaps dominant, roles. Many of these service and management specialists will be members of professional bodies, thus having direct responsibilities beyond those of an employee to an employer (albeit an employer that is a governmental body) – to the public at large. The for-profit and non-profit organisations contracted by governments will include similar professionally qualified staff, often from the same professional bodies.

Modern governments have always worked with for-profit organisations, especially in the procurement of goods, military or civilian. However, working with for-profits in wider senses, and with non-profit organisations, has developed in recent decades, under umbrella terms such as 'public–private partnerships' or just 'partnerships'. A major example throughout the UK government during the 1990s was known as the Private Finance Initiative, which was a wider approach than had been the case in the past by governmental organisations to using the private sector for capital projects. This development itself provided only the general parameters, leaving the contract between each pair of organisations (governmental organisation and for-profit organisation) to determine the specific details.

To understand the essence of the Private Finance Initiative, consider a common way for government to manage a capital project – say, the building of a hospital. The government determines the hospital that it wants and can afford (perhaps with the help of private sector architects and other consultants), invites tenders from companies that build hospitals, awards the contract to the best tender, then borrows the money (from the private sector) to pay the contractor to build it. The company builds the hospital and, on completion, hands over the keys to the government, which staffs and otherwise enables the hospital to provide hospital services. The government operates the hospital, ultimately financed by taxation. Principal and interest on the borrowing is similarly financed, ultimately, by taxation. In this way of providing hospital services, the private sector has played very important roles, but, once the hospital opens, it is the government and taxpayers that bear almost all of the risks and rewards ('almost all' because of the possibility of residual claims on the private sector contractors).

The essence of the Private Finance Initiative is to increase the use of private sector contractors. The early stages of the project may have been the same but, instead of then inviting tenders from companies that build hospitals, the government could invite tenders from companies that build, provide the capital finance for and operate hospitals (with the operating aspect limited, say, to the physical building and equipment). In such a case, once the hospital has been built, the keys would be held jointly by the contractors (who would maintain the building and the equipment) and the government (who would provide the doctors, nurses and managers). In return for providing the hospital building and equipment, the contractor would receive a fixed payment from the government, every year for (say) 30 years. At the end of the 30 years, the payments would stop and the building and equipment would be taken over by the government.

The economic essence of such a project, compared to a traditional project, is the shift in risk and reward to the private sector. As there are important parts of the projects that continue to be owned by the government, some of the explicit risks and rewards are retained by the public sector (as well as the implicit risks and rewards of all projects that are 'too big to fail'). The premise of these projects is that the services provided are better than those provided in a traditional project, because there is a better sharing of risk and reward between the public and private sectors. The risks and rewards in the private sector are, by their nature, expected to be higher; the risks for management in the public sector are expected to be lower, insulated from risk by the resort to taxation, and perhaps then the rewards are more typically lower, too. On the other hand, governments would not want the rewards to accrue to the private sector while the risks are borne by government. This risk sharing also emphasises the importance of risk management through the internal control system.

There were many such projects, with variations in detail. Indeed, there were periods when this was the only significant method for new capital projects in the UK public sector, and hundreds of billions of pounds have been involved in total. The popularity of these types of projects extended to other countries. The general idea of increasing the use of contractual relationships between governments and for-profit and not-for-profit organisations has become generically known as public–private partnerships, which have many different detailed forms.

Two fundamental issues in public management are whether there are, and should be, differences between public and private management. Neither issue is well understood. Most of the literature on management theory concerns for-profit organisations (even if, in important cases, it learned from governments). Public management theory is substantively much newer and is, by its own lights, confused. If we take the modern form of government as beginning towards the end of the nineteenth century (when the provision of public services – beyond that of waging war – became the norm), then, for most of that period, 'public administration' was the traditional term, with 'management' usually being reserved for for-profit organisations; governments and not-for-profits were 'administered'.

The terminology, in some cases, reflected the profoundly different concepts and practices of the public and private sectors. A clear example was national governments that saw and organised themselves in a fundamentally different way from a business. A major case is the continental European tradition of a civil service, reflected best in countries such as France and Germany, in which the administration (and management) of government is fundamentally a matter of law, carried out largely by lawyers, whereas business the world over (and government of the UK and the USA), while subject to law, is not carried out by it. Another major case was the UK government's eschewing of professional qualifications in favour of non-vocational degrees and learning by doing ('sitting next to Nelly') for its civil service. However, these cases of polarisation were not exclusive: in some countries' local government, possibly because of the localness and lack of sovereignty, there traditionally did tend to be a freer flow of expertise between government and the private sector professional bodies than was the case elsewhere.

On the issue of whether there are differences between public and private management, there have been clear specific cases of significant change in public management, which have tended towards the collapsing of differences between public and private management theory and practice. The increasing predomin-ance of the term 'public management' does suggest that there continue to be real differences between public and private management theory and practice. On the other hand, there is also evidence that there have been specific changes which have tended towards the collapsing of differences. Nevertheless, the public management theory literature is very tentative in its generalisations about what changed, when and where.

In the UK during the 1970s and 1980s, some clear examples of change contributed to the invention of the term 'new public management'. This term remains particularly unhelpful (even if it became very popular in some quarters), especially because it implies that there was an 'old public management' – a term that did not and still does not exist. More importantly, the attempt to generalise from the specific cases, which were drawn from the UK and other developed commonwealth countries, had less relevance to the USA (perhaps because there were earlier clear examples of the influence of business on government) and to continental Europe (perhaps because of the dominance of law in administration). Nevertheless, as the specific cases gained influence around the world, the term gained popularity in some quarters and it has been the focus of a significant amount of literature in academic accounting.

1.3 Public finance

Governments, for-profit and non-profit organisations all have the same forms of finance available to them, with the notable exception of government's right to tax, but there are different emphases placed on the kinds of finance in each type of organisation. Borrowing, short-term and long-term, is important for all types, as are reserves. Government grants (of all forms, including exemptions from payments to government) are important for all types of public and private organisations, even for national governments (who receive from other governments or governmental agencies); some grants have no specific restrictions on how the money is to be spent, while others have such restrictions. All types receive donations, some of which, again, have no specific restrictions on how the money is to be spent, while others have. Equity investment is available to all because even governments and not-for-profits can own or control for-profit organisations.

In the definitive senses, the emphasis in a government's balance sheet is on borrowing and grants; in a for-profit's balance sheet, on equity and borrowing; in a non-profit's, on donations. All types of organisations charge for goods and services (granting of rights, sales of products and services) but, in their definitive forms, governments and non-profits charge at or below full cost, while for-profits recover full costs (to include profit). These definitive forms are far from exclusive, of course: governments sell rights for as much as the market will bear and recover full costs of public housing; non-profits sell donated goods and services; and for-profits give away goods and services. The definitive forms, however, are more typical of the respective operating statements.

The irreducible difference in the financing of all these types of organisations is between those that can tax and those that cannot. Of those that can tax, there are the special cases of national governments (and a supranational government such as the European Union) in which the power to tax is exercised to not only finance the provision of public services but also manage the whole economy.

Finance for a national government can usefully be thought of, ultimately, as a pool of money provided by taxation. Accounting systems often have an account that reflects this. The fisc is a (now rarely used) term for this pool; fiscal (as in 'fiscal policy') is the adjective. Lending to a national government is, ultimately, secured on this pool and the right of the government to replenish the pool with taxation. In most governments of the world, this lending is taken to be default-free. It is not taken to be risk-free, though, because of the risk of changes in the value of money (though this might be mitigated to some extent if the debt is linked to a measure of general price inflation). It is taken to be free from default because taxpayers will pay interest on the debt and repay it. Taxpayers – not lenders – bear the financial risks of government. At national level, this means not just the risks of providing the government's own services and products but also the risks of those of state and local governments, for-profit organisations and non-profit organisations that cannot be allowed to fail.

In cases where state and local governments can borrow from the market, the question arises about the extent to which the lenders are bearing these risks, a particularly important question for the national governments and their central banks that may end up bearing them. Generally, the European practice is for the lending to be either explicitly default-free (because the national government explicitly guarantees the debt) or implicitly so (because the national government would not allow a state or local government to default). The same is common in the USA, but, alongside, it is the norm for its state and local governments to issue debt that is explicitly *not* free from default. As a result, there is a long-standing, and much more significant, industry in the credit rating of state and local government debt in the USA.

These central pools of public money, in addition to bearing ultimate risks, also provide finance to state and local governments, for-profit and non-profit organisations, which give the national governments significant powers over them. The extent of those powers, and how they are exercised, varies widely. In the case of state and local governments, it is typical for them to be dependent on grants from this central pool and, in many countries, the local tax base is so small in relation to these grants, and their ability to borrow so small, that the local 'governments' might better be thought of as local arms of the sovereign governments. In the case of for-profit organisations that are not allowed to fail, the powers might be so great as effectively to render them nationalised.

Borrowing by governments, secured as it is explicitly or implicitly on taxation, has a special dimension to it: this year's taxpayers are not the same as next and subsequent years', raising the question of intergenerational equity for the different generations of taxpayers. Current taxpayers may not have the incentives to be concerned about the taxpayers of future years and politicians are endowed with finite, and short, time horizons by the electoral system. The orthodoxy of unbalanced budgets in situations in which the imperative is to balance the national economy necessarily weakens financial control in the sense that it allows the current taxpayers to have the benefits from spending but not pay for them. Accounting systems and other financial disciplines attempt to re-establish the link – for example, with strict balanced budget requirements or pay-as-you-go requirements that relate to individual incremental spending proposals having to be accompanied by specific savings elsewhere.

1.4 Public money

For an accountant, the starting point for understanding the term 'public money' is that the accountant is handling other people's money, which brings power, of course, but also great responsibilities. However, most accountants in for-profit organisations and non-profit organisations also handle other people's money: in the long-standing phrase, ownership has long been typically divorced from control.

Public money is more than just other people's money, though: it is money taken compulsorily from taxpayers. In a functioning system, there must be general consent from taxpayers as a whole to pay taxes, but, in every individual case, the taxpayer has the duty to pay the tax bill issued, enforceable in the courts, regardless of this general consent. Moreover, because the public services are typically provided to service recipients free at the point of delivery, the spending of public money does not itself generate more revenues (as spending in a profitable business does): it just generates more tax bills. In this, it is similar to a non-profit organisation as its spending generates more demand for voluntary donations – but donations, not taxes.

People's demands for more services and products appear to be limitless, regardless of who the supplier is, whether government, for-profit or non-profit. Whereas in the for-profit case, though, the demands have to be paid for by each individual, in the other two cases the demands are deliberately separated, in each individual's case, from paying for them. In the non-profit case, there is no specific right of each individual to have the demands satisfied, but in the case of government, there often is, defined by law.

The accountant's responsibility for public money comes down to the responsibility to force individuals and individual for-profit organisations to pay, continuously and continually, taxes that are used to satisfy demands, often developing into rights, for services free at the point of delivery. It is a special form of stewardship, in which the stewards are the accountants (primarily concerned with money) and the rest of the managers (primarily concerned with the services provided). These stewards are responsible to the public, in the end, but, within each government, they are responsible to the public's representatives – that is, politicians endowed – in a democracy – with finite, and short, time horizons to the next election. The long-term power of these public representatives depends on the next set of votes, each of which is, by its nature, a crude measure of each voter's preference for services and taxes. In stumping for votes, the politician is offering to each voter the promise of services free at the point of delivery (good) and a tax bill (bad). If the politician can separate these, by borrowing to pay for the services in the short term or otherwise reduce the short-term tax, there are natural incentives for the votes to be forthcoming. Particular, and recurring, forms of political corruption blossom in this separation: a prestige project or a very local project, with a politician's name attached, that yields sufficient local votes but is out of kilter with other projects.

The accountant, when a career public official, has a long time horizon and, being concerned primarily with money, functions in the now technically complex world of money itself and what money is used to measure (revenues, expenses, assets, liabilities and cash flows). To the accountant, no services are free at the point of delivery: all have to be paid for by taxation, sooner or later. The accountant's longer time horizon provides natural incentives to try and capture the long-term effects on taxation of short-term borrowing and communicate these to taxpayers as a whole. In other words, there are clear incentives for accountants as stewards to want to override the people's representatives – perhaps even the people. These are in addition to the incentives that accountants in all organisations have to want to override their fellow non-financial managers. All groups in society appeal to the public interest, but the public interest appeal of accountants in relation to public money has special dimensions, including what can sometimes seem like piety.

Common consequences have been the desire for accountants to have central control of public money, whether the 'centre' is the centre of a local, state or national government, insulated from overt political influence. It is anyway a truth of government – however disturbing – that the more technical a matter is, the less will be the political understanding of and influence over it. The extent to which the desire has been achieved in different settings at different times has varied widely, as is to be expected. Some governments will emphasise the greater importance of political accountability; over time, the importance of the career officials will wax and wane, as the relative wealth of the government changes. Professional accounting bodies, never questioning that ultimate power should be in the hands of politicians, tend to represent this desire.

A common effect on the control of public money of the separation between providing services and paying for them has been that of encouraging governments to buy cheaply – even to buy the cheapest – in the markets, regardless of how wealthy the country is. The most enduring specific manifestation if this is in rules requiring the lowest tenders from contractors to be accepted. More concrete examples are austere public offices occupied by public officials on low salaries, alongside plush private offices and managers with the salaries to match. Public money has often signalled parsimony, regardless of the effects on the services provided.

The written statements of ethics for government accountants are not different, in their generalities, from the equivalents for those in the private sector. Equity or fairness would be judged differently, though, as it is in the nature of public money to be more often and more acutely concerned with the public interest.

1.5 Accountants and the public sector

The accounting discipline is a product of the accounting profession (not of universities), which formally began in the UK and the USA in the second half of the nineteenth century. What is now the Institute of Chartered Accountants in

England and Wales was formed in 1880 and what is now the American Institute of Certified Public Accountants in 1887. The profession's emergence coincided with the expansion of government services at national level, essentially from defence to all aspects of welfare, with a parallel increase in welfare provision at state and local government levels. The accounting profession grew, however, by providing services for businesses, not for governments and non-profits.

The traditional accounting techniques of recording, measuring and communicating, typically using money, form the basis of the cognitive skills necessary for the accounting profession's success. These are not sufficient (because judgement is an important part of accounting expertise), but they are necessary. They provide a fundamental reason for the accounting profession having had less influence over government than it does on business in the private sector because accounting technique itself has less influence in governments than it does on the private sector.

To illustrate the point, imagine two comparable hospitals using the same accounting software to record and measure revenues, expenses, assets, liabilities and cash flows, but with one difference: one is a governmental organisation, financed by taxation, while the other is financed by charges (either for-profit or non-profit). The accounting system in the governmental hospital would tell us much less about that hospital than would be revealed by the accounting system in the hospital financed by charges. That is because the same software would, in the former, not provide us with that fundamental measure of performance, return on capital, but, in the latter, it would (even if it were a non-profit, because the return on capital would be a fundamental measure of performance at break-even). We might decide that more use of accounting in the governmental hospital would produce better hospitals and, therefore, we might, in the place of taxation, construct revenue streams that proxy what patients, or their insurance companies, would pay for the services. That would significantly increase the importance of accounting in the governmental hospital, though, presumably, not to the level of importance it has in the for-profit hospital.

As well as accounting technique itself having less influence in governments, in a basic sense government accounting technique is of less interest to voters than accounting technique in a public company is to its equivalent owners, the equity investors. Voters have no significant economic incentive to understand government accounting technique because rational voters necessarily depend on simple factors and accounting technique is not simple. Rational voters do not even have the economic incentive to pay experts to analyse government accounting technique on their behalf. Equity investors, on the other hand, have strong economic incentives to understand the accounting techniques of the businesses they own, or might own, and pay well for the services of financial analysts. In this sense, government accounting is largely insulated from the general population, relative at least to business accounting, as the environment is fundamentally different.

There are also what we might call institutional reasons for the relative lack of influence of the professional accounting bodies in government. The bodies are themselves in the private sector, even if their members have benefited from special recognition by their host governments (especially by restricting statutory audits of companies to their members) and if there has been increasing regulation of their work by public bodies. The core values of these professional bodies, and their umbrella bodies such as the International Federation of Accountants, are that:

- the bodies themselves are non-profit organisations (by legal and tax definitions), though the individual and firm members of these bodies are for-profit
- this non-profit status imposes on the bodies, and each firm and individual member, duties to society as a whole and not just to the members' clients
- the majority of their members are not employed by their clients but work on contract for them
- even when a member is so employed, that person or firm still has wider duties to the public interest
- the accounting and auditing judgements of the bodies, and of the firms and individual members, are ostensibly apolitical, in the sense of not being overtly influenced by government, either by its politicians or its civil servants.

As the professional accounting bodies are, to varying degrees, recognised by their host governments, those governments share these values – as they relate to accounting and auditing services provided to for-profit and non-profits. However, most governments, most of the time since the formation of these bodies, have not shared these values in accounting and auditing the governments themselves, at least not to the same extent. This is especially true in national governments. In one obvious sense, it is also easy to understand: being ostensibly apolitical in a government is, for many, undesirable and, for those who desire it, especially difficult to succeed at. Accounting and auditing depend on much routine, technical matter, but this can never be completely separated from policy questions.

Governments, rather than employing professional accountants, tended to look to generic administrators to carry out their financial functions – civil servants, public servants, local government officials. Moreover, government budgeting, especially in the finance ministries of sovereign governments (UK Treasury, US Office of Management and Budget), is not primarily a function of accounting but, rather, of economics and policy analysis; and the economists and statisticians of statistical offices have important roles in measuring government economic activity.

There was one significant, though now small, exception to the preference for generic administrators over professional accountants. In UK local government, the finance officials created their own branch of the nascent accounting profession, in 1885, as an institute that soon became an examining and certifying body, and that currently exists as the Chartered Institute of Public Finance and Accountancy. Relative to the rest of the accounting profession, the body remains small, not least because local government itself has lost many of its historic functions. In the USA, a similar organisation, currently known as the Government Finance Officers Association, was established in 1906 at the state and local government level. This body is of importance, but it is not an examining and certifying accounting body. Those who carry out accounting functions in government might be, and increasingly have been, qualified accountants, but these would typically have had little, even no, education and training in public sector accounting.

The tension between the dual responsibilities of professional accountants and auditors employed – even contracted – by governments has never been easy to reconcile and is not well understood. It is easy to state that their responsibilities to their profession and to their governmental employer are ultimately to the same public and are ultimately therefore the same. Those responsibilities, however, are mediated by organisations that are fundamentally different. The professional accounting bodies are in the private sector and are expected to function as such, with the concomitant expectation that if they are unsuccessful in private sector terms, they will perish.

There is one overt sense in which the values of the accounting profession have come to challenge governments at the highest levels. The most visible change in the profession in the second half of the twentieth century has been the emergence of codified sets of accounting for published financial statements, which are at the core of generally accepted accounting practice (GAAP, adopted in the UK mainly from the 1990s onwards). The USA took the lead in this, for public companies – a lead that is traceable to the public regulation of the stock exchanges starting from 1933/1934, though the first policymaker (recognisable as such today) would date from the establishment by the accounting profession of the Accounting Principles Board in 1959. The modern equivalents are the Financial Accounting Standards Board (for the USA) and the International Accounting Standards Board, though these bodies are formally separate from the professional accounting bodies. These codified sets of accounting are typically, in the public companies, audited by members of the professional accounting bodies.

At the heart of this influential accounting and auditing is the requirement that the accounting policies are set by a private sector (non-profit) body, formally independent of the accounting profession and independent of the companies preparing the financial statements, with compliance by those financial statements being judged, in the first instance, by auditors in the private sector who are responsible to their professional accounting bodies (and, in the USA, to a public body), which are also independent of the companies being audited.

This challenges many, if not most, governments because the traditional practice has been for national governments to set their own accounting policies, compliance with which is judged by auditors who are not in the private sector and, in a number of cases, are in the governments themselves. In lower-level governments, the challenges are fewer because the higher-level government can set the policies and require an independent audit. We can see this distinction in the way that governments have responded to the changes in the accounting profession.

The first major use of codifications for governments followed the formation in the USA of the Governmental Accounting Standards Board in 1984 – a private sector body that makes policies for state and local governments and is formally independent of them and the accounting profession. In 1990, in the USA, the Federal Accounting Standards Advisory Board was established to develop a codification for accounting at the federal level. This body cannot be judged to be independent of the federal government, however. In 2004, the world's professional accounting bodies, in the form of the International Federation of Accountants based in New York City, established the International Public Sector Accounting Standards Board (IPSASB) (with predecessor committees dating from 1986), to develop a codification for accounting and reporting by governments of the world – though these standards were to have no power in themselves, each government being free to accept or reject them. All of these codifications were developed in English (even if, in the case of international public sector accounting standards [IPSAS], they were subsequently translated).

The emergence of the IPSASB followed from the most radical change ever in public sector accounting (early in the 1990s): the adoption by sovereign governments of a comprehensive form of accrual accounting. Lower-level governments had had a longer exposure to accrual accounting and, with differing impacts in different countries, had adopted modified forms. Sovereign governments had, however, for as long as there had been an accounting profession and for much longer before that, adopted cash-based systems that almost exclusively focused on execution of the budget. The adoption of any form of accrual accounting was a very radical change indeed.

Notwithstanding the existence of these bodies, the usual case is of a national government that makes its own accounting policies, presumably including this right as part of its sovereignty over many other matters. Great diversity in the theory and practice of government accounting is therefore the norm, not least because most of the governments in the world do not account in English. The pervasive influence of common software packages, often modified from the for-profit context, might be reducing some of this diversity.

The codified sets of accounting do present a challenge to governments all the same, if only because common sense suggests (to the point where voters might respond to the suggestion) that organisations should not be accountable against their own accounting rules. A weakness in the challenge is that these codified sets of accounting are limited to codified sets of financial reporting, mostly ignoring budgets. Budgets are as important in businesses as in any other kind of organisation and have long so been. When management accounting in business was being developed as a subdiscipline of accounting in the USA in the 1920s, it was significantly influenced by the introduction of budgeting to the federal government there. The practice of governments disclosing their budgets did not transfer to business. Thus, financial reporting for businesses, reflected in the codified sets of accounting, mainly ignores budgets and is restricted to the financial statements (mainly the operating statement, balance sheet and cash flow statement). In governments, as important as the financial statements may be, budgets are the primary financial reports. The accounting rules for these budgets are also typically made by the governments themselves. So, while there is a challenge to the financial statements, there is very little challenge to the budgets. To accountants, this is troublesome because budgets are seen to be an inextricable part of the accounting cycle, even if, in businesses, they are usually confidential. A fact of governmental life is that budgets commonly use a different accounting basis from the financial statements, which the codified sets of financial reporting are hardly going to change.

This Anglo-American (often, in continental Europe, termed Anglo-Saxon) tradition, has an extra challenge to the continental European view of civil service, reflected best and most influentially in countries such as France and Germany. In those countries, the administration (or management) of government is fundamentally a matter of law, carried out largely by lawyers. The Anglo-American tradition is subject to law, of course, but is not carried out by it.

Identifying this Anglo-American tradition is useful, as long as we are also always alert to differences between the UK and the USA. In business accounting in the two countries, the biggest difference was the tendency for standards in the USA to include significantly more detail in the measurement rules and disclosure requirements (the so-called rules-based approach) than in UK and International Standards (the principles-based or concepts-based approach). In government accounting, however, the differences between the two countries are much greater, especially at the highest level of government, which in the USA is similar to influential continental European systems.

Researching and teaching accounting dramatically increased in the 1970s, including in universities. In this, the term 'public sector accounting' was increasingly used. In the USA, however, the term 'government and non-profit' came to be preferred, with the latter being segregated into those non-profits deemed private (notwithstanding their tax benefits) and those clearly belonging to or otherwise associated with governments.

The lack of a specific status for public sector accounting is also reflected in the absence of a generally accepted term for those who carry it out. 'Public accountant' might have been the most obvious candidate, except that it had already become entrenched as the term for an accountant who provided services (definitively including audit) to businesses on contract, not as employees – hence, they are said to be in public practice, their services available to all. The term is, of course, enshrined in the US designation of Certified Public Accountant.

All accounting is arcane to anyone other than accountants, suffering as it does from the lack of a generally accepted dictionary and, thus, the proliferation of inconsistent usage of terms. For public sector accounting, this is even more the case, given that most teaching and learning of accounting begins with the inconsistent terms of for-profit accounting, extended, if they are at all, to governments.

FURTHER READING

Bac, A. (ed.) (2001) *International Comparative Issues in Government Accounting*, Kluwer.

Bourgon, J. (2007) 'Responsive, responsible and respected government: towards a new public administration theory', *International Review of Administrative Sciences*, 73(1): 7–26, with a response from Rexed, K. (2008), 74(1): 131–43.

Bourmistrov, A. and Mellemvik, F. (eds) (2005) *International Trends and Experiences in Government Accounting*, Oslo: Cappelen Akademisk Forlag.

Broadbent, J. and Guthrie, J. (2008) 'Public sector to public services: 20 years of "contextual" accounting research', *Accounting, Auditing and Accountability Journal*, 21(2): 129–69.

Broadbent, J. and Laughlin, R. (2005) 'The role of PFI in the UK government's modernization agenda', *Financial Accountability and Management*, 21(1): 75–97.

Buschor, E. and Schedler, K. (eds) (1994) *Perspectives on Performance Measurement and Public Sector Accounting*, Berne: Haupt.

Clarke, P. and Lapsley, I. (2004) 'Management accounting in the new public sector', *Management Accounting Research*, 15: 243–5.

Ferlie, E., Lynn, L. and Pollitt, C. (eds) (2005) *The Oxford Handbook of Public Management*, Oxford University Press.

Gualmini, E. (2008) 'Restructuring Weberian bureaucracy: comparing managerial reforms in Europe and the United States', *Public Administration*, 86(1): 75–94.

Hartley, J., Donaldson, C., Skelcher, C. and Wallace, M. (eds) (2008) *Managing to Improve Public Services*, Cambridge University Press.

Jorge, S. (ed.) (2008) *Implementing Reforms in Public Sector Accounting*, Portugal: Imprensa da Universidade Coimbra.

Kaufmann, F., Majone, G. and Ostrom, V. (eds) (1986) *Guidance, Control, and Evaluation in the Public Sector*, Berlin and New York: de Gruyter.

Lande, E. and Scheid, J.-C. (eds) (2006) *Accounting Reform in the Public Sector: Mimicry, Fad or Necessity*, Paris: Experts Comptables Media.

Lapsley, I. (2009) 'New public management: the cruellest invention of the human spirit?', *Abacus*, 45(1): 1–21.

Montesinos, V. and Vela, J-M. (eds) (2002) *Innovations in Governmental Accounting*, Kluwer.

Newberry, S. (ed.) (2007) *The Legacy of June Pallot*, Information Age Publishing.

Power, M. (2009) 'The risk management of nothing', *Accounting, Organizations and Society*, 34: 849–55.

van Helden, J. (2005) 'Researching public sector transformation: the role of management accounting', *Financial Accountability and Management*, 21(1): 99–133.

Chapter 2

Performance measurement

Services provided free at the point of delivery and financed by taxation are the distinctive concern of public sector accounting. If the services were sold in competitive markets, sales revenues would provide financial measures of how much the service users valued the services delivered: income measurement, the province of accounting, would be a relevant performance measure. Tax revenues cannot provide such measures. The unrelenting demand for performance measurement in the public sector is met with non-financial measures. These kinds of measures provide distinctive challenges for public sector accounting.

2.1 Non-financial performance measurement

Governments exist to govern; how they perform is a matter of legal, political, economic, social and historical judgements. These judgements might refer to their performance during historically significant periods, such as war, or of a major policy, such as a national health service, or of a particular term of office of a political party or a political leader. In making these judgements, data are naturally used and sometimes measured, depending on the particular methodology adopted.

Performance measurement, in this context, refers to a much more specific sense of performance than the above. It requires governments to see important aspects of governing as the provision of specific services, in definitive form free at the point of delivery, to specific individuals or groups of individuals. This sense of specificity is sometimes enhanced by referring to the services provided as 'products'. Performance measurement requires the planning, execution and monitoring of the government's service provision to include measurement of the specific services.

The more these specific services can plausibly be reduced to products, the more relevant the performance measurement will be. A hip replacement for a 62-year-old woman cannot be treated wholly separately from all other aspects of her health but it still useful to do so. Such products can be identified as separable parts of the health services that the government, for-profit and non-profit organisations provide but the services of those organisations cannot be wholly reduced to sets of products, much less can the health of the population, in all its dimensions.

The government services provided today are inseparable from those provided in the past and, given that security, health and education are of the most fundamental cultural kind, from the long distant past. The services provided by government organisations, again, because each is only contributing to the overall well-being of the population, are also inseparable from each other, and from the for-profit and non-profit organisations that also contribute. Performance measurement of an organisation, relating to the arbitrary period of a fiscal year, cannot naturally be separated from past performance or from the performance of others. This also means that the ideal of performance measurement of an organisation, namely to judge only those matters that are under the control of the organisation, cannot be achieved.

Moreover, the specificity of performance measurement requires the measures to be partial, which, in the absence of a unifying metric such as money, means that, taken together, they are necessarily incomplete. There is no complete set of performance measures – no absolute measure of performance of an organisation, a programme or a government as a whole. Sensible judgements of these measures are all comparative as they are about marginal changes over time and marginal differences between other organisations.

During the second half of the twentieth century there was a stream of initiatives in government budgeting and accounting that shared the same fundamental premise: given scarce resources, explicit measurement of the quantity – and, if possible, the quality – of services provided, linked to the measurement of resources consumed produces better services. In the 1950s and 1960s, the initiatives produced the comprehensive budgeting models known as performance budgeting, programme budgeting and zero-base budgeting. In the 1970s and 1980s, the initiatives focused more on auditing and, since then, the focus has been on every aspect of budgeting, accounting and auditing.

This premise can be said to underpin all for-profit organisations: the resources consumed and the quantity and quality of services provided are measured using money. As money is the medium of accounting, accounting has a central role in performance measurement in for-profits.

It is useful at this point to distinguish two senses of money. First, money is the primary medium of exchange and thereby a primary store of wealth. Accounting records the exchange transactions and the concomitant changes in wealth; sometimes the monetary transactions involve cash and (slightly less liquid) near cash, but, more often, claims to cash (receivables and payables, short-term and long-term loans). Accounting aggregates these records of transactions, but then uses money to produce refined measures of revenues, expenses, assets, liabilities and cash flows. Put another way, this aggregation and measurement distinguishes between operating amounts (relating to a year or shorter period) and capital amounts (longer than a year).

In any organisation, accounting provides measures of performance, in the sense of measures of whether the changes in revenues, expenses, assets, liabilities and cash flows during the period were as expected. In a for-profit organisation, however, accounting's use of money also provides a direct measure of the value of goods and services provided. The fact that the operating revenues are willingly paid by customers in competitive markets means that those revenues are objective measures of what the for-profit provides. Cash flows in to and out of the entity, including distinctions between operating and capital flows, provide important measures of the success of the entity. Revenues minus expenses, expressed as a percentage of capital employed, however, are an even more fundamental measure of the performance of the entity – of its ability to use resources (labour, materials, property, plant and equipment, money) to satisfy the need for its goods and services.

The obvious advantage that money has (over bartering or other non-monetary methods, such as political influence) is that it provides a common measure of all transactions between for-profit organisations and all other organisations and individuals, however intrinsically different the goods and services provided may be. This universal metric is used by each of us in making our choices about satisfying our needs, and by those organisations that provide for our needs. We all know, to a great or lesser degree, that money transactions cannot satisfy all our needs and they often cannot even capture everything about a product or service in a given transaction (because each of us has different amounts of money and markets fail). Yet these exchange transactions using money are powerful and have provided accounting with vicarious power, especially in for-profit organisations, in which money captures so much.

When services are provided free at the point of delivery, the recipients do not express their preferences by accepting or rejecting a price for the services. Money does not, therefore, provide an observable measure of the services and products provided. The other uses of money are common to government, however – in particular, money provides an observable measure of what the organisation buys in order to provide a service. Money has additional uses in measuring the government's ability to collect taxes, by comparing money collected with what was budgeted to be collected.

In definitive governments, in which the services provided free at the point of delivery are financed by taxation, performance is assessed using financial and non-financial measures and qualitative judgements. In performance measurement, it is useful to think of the following distinct elements of performance:

- inputs, being resources consumed by the government, measured primarily using costs but also non-financial measures – commonly, the number of employees
- outputs, being the services provided, measured primarily using non-financial measures
- outcomes, also being the services provided, but primarily using unmeasured, qualitative judgements, though when the judgements of outcomes are systematically gathered from service recipients, typically based on interviews or questionnaires, they can be measured and statistics of satisfaction produced.

Non-financial inputs, outputs and outcomes of government services are best thought of as being hierarchical. At the low levels of the hierarchy there are easily counted surrogate measures of input, while at the higher levels there are easily counted surrogate measures of output, then easily counted output measures, then counted measures of service recipient satisfaction and, at the highest level, unmeasurable outcomes. The lowest levels in the hierarchy, while they can be reliably measured, are furthest away from what the government services are ultimately trying to achieve; at the highest level they are what the services are ultimately trying to achieve, but cannot be measured.

None of the levels in the hierarchy of outputs and outcomes is the natural responsibility of accounting. In the provision of government services (as in non-profits), outputs and outcomes are matters for others – in this case, service professionals and politicians. That includes the measurement of outputs and outcomes. Such measurement can be easy and related to matters of fact, but questions of what to measure, how to measure and what use to make of the resultant measures are not neutral, so accountants are not free to answer them.

Nevertheless, accounting is acutely interested in those outputs and outcomes. Performance measurement is meaningless to accounting without consideration of what the services cost. Performance is usefully analysed into inputs, outputs and outcomes, but all of these elements must be judged together. Successful outputs and outcomes at any cost are not useful measures of performance (number and classification of examination passes increase, as do approval levels, but budgets are overspent and borrowing is out of control); successful outputs, with unsuccessful outcomes, at high cost are not either (number and classification of examination passes increase, but approval levels fall and budgets are overspent and borrowing is out of control). In the short term, accounting might judge successful outputs, with unsuccessful outcomes but at low cost, favourably (number and classification of examination passes increase, but approval levels fall and budgets are lowest compared with comparable services), but in the medium term might worry about the implications for future budgets if the low approval levels lead to radical changes.

The language of financial and non-financial inputs, non-financial outputs and outcomes is commonly expressed in different ways. For example, distinguishing between economy, efficiency and effectiveness. Economy focuses on financial inputs, to judge whether the costs were as low as possible. It is bolstered by the sense that public money must be spent on the cheapest option. Efficiency is a ratio of inputs to outputs, measurable in financial or non-financial terms. Effectiveness here focuses on whether the outputs and outcomes ultimately achieved what was wanted or not. A common way to use these terms is to point out that a programme could be very efficient but ineffective: it could do the wrong things very well. In ordinary usage, we would not say that something was efficient if it was doing the wrong thing, but, in this technical sense, we might say so and separating the terms can help to reinforce the point. They can also be used, however, to emphasise how imperative it is to judge economy, efficiency and effectiveness together. The age-old imperative to spend public money on the cheapest that money can buy never made sense when buying cheaply meant buying unwisely.

To illustrate all of the aspects of performance measurement, take the example of secondary school education. Exhibit 2.1 gives the performance measures for Secondary School A in Eutopia.

Exhibit 2.1 Secondary School A, City of Eutopia: Education Department's performance measures

School A's budget for 20x2 is £3,000,000. In 20x2, it has 450 students and 70 full-time teachers. It is one of four secondary schools in Eutopia, each with 500 places. The annual operating budget for 20x2 for secondary schools within the Education Department of the city is £10,000,000. There are 1950 students and 350 full-time teachers in total. In all schools, in addition to the full-time teachers, part-time teachers and teaching assistants are used.

All secondary schools in the country are subject to national testing for students aged 14 and 16. The national tests for 14-year-olds are in English, mathematics and science and are marked as A, B or C. The national tests for 16-year-olds are in these and many other subjects, each student typically taking at least eight subjects, and the tests are similarly marked as A, B or C.

In 20x2, School A's results in the tests for 14-year-olds were English 55 per cent A, 15 per cent B and 30 per cent C; mathematics 60 per cent A, 15 per cent B and 25 per cent C; science 60 per cent A, 10 per cent B and 30 per cent C; and for 16-year-olds were 45 per cent gaining five or more A or B grades.

The surrogate measure of financial input is the number of teachers and the surrogate measures of output are the number of students. The direct measures of output are numbers of examination passes at different levels of success. These measures are just one part of the teaching and learning experience in secondary schools, which, in turn, is one part of students' educational experience, from primary through to higher education.

Exhibit 2.2 provides the local and national background to the funding of the services provided by School A.

Exhibit 2.2 Local and national background to performance of Secondary School A, City of Eutopia: funding

There are 2000 secondary schools (for students aged 11–19) in the whole of the country, ranging from schools that provide 250 places to those that provide 1000 places. The national government has an overall responsibility for secondary school education, including the national testing at ages of 14 and 16. It also provides substantial funding, across a range of initiatives but also for a large proportion of its annual operating expenditure, which is distributed to each of the cities and then to each school. The formula for distribution is based on student numbers, but also includes other factors, such as local living costs (because these affect the purchasing power of teachers' salaries), the percentage of students who receive free school meals (because this is a measure of relative poverty) and the percentage of students whose first language is not Eutopian (because this is a measure of possible special learning difficulties).

The national government's budget for secondary school education will increase substantially over the next three years, but, because of the complexity of the revenue streams into each secondary school, it is not possible to know in 20x2 how each school's budget will be affected.

School A is almost wholly dependent on the national government for its funding and the testing that determines the performance measures of the school, in terms of the methods of testing, what to test and how. The actual results of every student are determined on behalf of the national government by an agency and those results are the definitive ones. The school receives a copy of the results for all of its students.

The national government explicitly knows that there are factors relevant to the performance of a school other than the numbers of A, B and C grades achieved by its students. These factors are relevant to the measures of input (local living costs of teachers) and of output (poverty and learning difficulties of students) and are used in determining funding, but they are not part of the performance measurement.

The complexity of the funding of secondary schools means that it is not possible for the national government to link inputs, outputs and outcomes comprehensively when the budgets are fixed and, therefore, when they are executed and monitored. The increments of the budgets for 20x2 to 20x5 can be linked to incremental changes in the performance measures, as in Exhibit 2.3.

Exhibit 2.3 Local and national background to performance of Secondary School A, City of Eutopia: national government's performance measures

The national government has set a strategic objective to increase the number of students in each category, in the two sets of examinations, by 2 percentage points a year between 20x2 and 20x5. The consequent performance measures set by the national government for 20x2 are, for 14-year-olds, English, 75 per cent A, 20 per cent B and 5 per cent C; mathematics 75 per cent A, 20 per cent B and 5 per cent C; science 80 per cent A, 15 per cent B and 5 per cent C. For 16-year-olds, they are 50 per cent gaining five or more A or B grades.

The measures are used to judge the performance of the national government in terms of meeting these targets. However, they are less satisfactory in judging the performance of each secondary school relative to all other schools. That is because the test results in one school are likely to be affected by factors that are not under the control of the school. The education specialists are not always agreed on what the factors are or their relative importance, but there is some agreement, as illustrated in Exhibit 2.4.

Exhibit 2.4 Local and national background to performance of Secondary School A, City of Eutopia: factors affecting performance in tests

A long-established independent national research body in education has established some of the factors, with a reasonable level of assurance, that affect test results. The quality of the education service provided in each school, which is under the control of each school, is supplemented by factors that are not under each school's control. These relate to the students and include prior academic achievement, their ethnicity, gender, age, special educational needs, relative poverty, first language not English, and the length of time spent enrolled in one school.

Some of these factors determine the distribution of national government grants (relative poverty and special educational needs), but others do not (prior academic achievement, ethnicity, gender, age, first language not English, and the length of time spent enrolled in one school) and none is overtly used to determine the overall budget for each secondary school.

The national government does need to understand the contribution that each school makes to its performance targets, including School A's, in its highly aggregated planning, execution and monitoring of the 2000 schools. One part of this is a government inspection service, illustrated in Exhibit 2.5.

Exhibit 2.5 Local and national background to performance of Secondary School A, City of Eutopia: performance inspection by national government

The national government has an inspection system under which a national government agency inspects each school every five years. The inspection takes a risk-based approach to assessing whether or not each school is outstanding, good, satisfactory or inadequate, which translates into a four-point scale, from 4 to 1 respectively. This overall judgement is based on more detailed judgements of schools' performance. The report is short and essentially qualitative, addressing matters such as whether or not the students feel safe, there is an ethos of student support and so on. The report is made public online. The last report for School A was in 20x0 and it was given a '3'.

The inspection reports are qualitative judgements of school outcomes, set in the context of reference to test results. The judgements emerge from visits to each school, including informal interviews with staff, students and parents, and are expressed in scores on a scale of 4 down to 1. The report for each school does not make reference to budgets, either financial or of numbers of employees.

For School A, and especially for its accountant, key parts of this elaborate performance measurement system are exogenous and determined only partially, leaving it up to the school to put all the parts together in offering the teaching and learning experience. Only the school's planning, execution and monitoring cycle explicitly takes a view of all the inputs, outputs and outcomes of the school – those key parts determined elsewhere, from above as it were.

The outcomes of a school are not only judged in educational terms. Exhibit 2.6 gives an example of another way of judging outcomes – the overall health of students.

Exhibit 2.6 Local and national background to performance of Secondary School A, City of Eutopia: a national government initiative to encourage healthy eating

The national government also has a programme to use school meals to increase healthy eating, in the first instance by students. After generations of school meals of low nutritional value, they are now very highly nutritious, though it is a challenge to get students to eat them. Free school meals are a part of this programme. The national government has determined, based on proxies not direct recordkeeping, that 40 per cent of students have school meals, 10 per cent are entitled to free meals but only 8 per cent take them up.

The school must determine how much the budget should be for healthy meals, how much this is an increase over the previous years' budgets for unhealthy eating, where to find the additional funds if the overall budget is not sufficient, how to increase the numbers of students eating school meals and how to pay for any increase in uptake of free school meals. It must also ensure that the incremental change in eating habits does not adversely affect all other aspects of students life, including their performance in tests.

The linking of inputs and outputs is typically done using long-standing surrogate measures:

- student–teacher ratio (output/input)
- cost per student (input/output).

These can be used by each school, the city and the national government to compare with previous years' and with other schools, cities or national governments. For cities and national governments, similar measures can usefully be produced relating to population size to compare with other cities and governments:

- number of secondary school teachers per 1000 population (input/output)
- cost of secondary schools per 1000 population (input/output).

Judging the performance of School A – even using the relatively limited number of measures given in Exhibits 2.1–2.6 – involves making sense of contradictory signals. School A clearly underperformed (see the test results in Exhibit 2.1) against the national targets (see Exhibit 2.3). Part of the explanation may have been some of the factors not under the school's control, such as prior academic achievement or ethnicity (see Exhibit 2.4). The school had a 'good' inspection report (see Exhibit 2.5, based on qualitative criteria) and may have done well on healthy eating (see Exhibit 2.6). The cost per student in School A (£6666 [£3m/450]) is higher than the average for Eutopia (£5128 [£10m/1950]). The student/teacher ratio is, on the other hand, also higher in School A (6.4:1 [450/70]) than the average in Eutopia (5.6:1 [1950/350]), though this measure does not take account of part-time teachers and teaching assistants. In the absence of a method for trading off these measures, within their own terms they are hard to rationalise overall.

All the performance measures are part of the teaching and learning experiences in the secondary schools, but these cannot be otherwise measured. That is why the measures are often referred to as *indicators* of performance, rather than the performance itself. The measures may be implemented in the control cycle because they are judged by the politicians, managers and teachers to be right for particular schools at particular points. The educational experience, however, is not understood to the point where there is general consensus about all elements of the experience. In that sense, we can say that the technology of education is not understood: to understand that we would have to have consensus on how each of our minds work, but, of course, we do not have such understanding.

A much-asserted characteristic (though supported by surprisingly little robust evidence) is that the participants in a service focus more on the measured aspects than the unmeasured, the hard not the soft. Caricatures (that may be commonly true) may portray the accountants as focusing on non-financial inputs, because they are not only measured but also provide good surrogates for costs, while students and their families and friends may be portrayed as focusing on examination success, necessarily encouraging the teachers to do the same, and the examiners may, similarly, be portrayed as focusing on examination success, when the examiners are independent of the teachers, which leaves the teachers and the rest of the general population, including employers and public intellectuals, to worry about the quality of education.

These principles of performance measurement are applied to all government services, but there is a special characteristic of education that typically does not apply to the others. The testing that provides the basis of the performance measurement has long been inherent to the system. In that way, performance measurement for educational organisations and programmes is able to draw on existing measures rather than having to invent them. This should be remembered in other contexts, although the challenges of performance measurement are less to do with the output measures themselves than with how they are used.

The obvious weaknesses of non-financial performance measurement continually invite ways of introducing money measures of outputs and outcomes to overcome them. Governments may choose to infer the price of a comparable service provided by a business, while the service recipient may choose to compare the free service with a comparable service provided for a fee (when possible), and a researcher might observe these inferences from data collected from questionnaires. Artificial markets – sometimes known as internal markets because they are internal to government or part of government – may be used to produce revenue streams that, even if they do not measure the willingness of ultimate recipients of the service to pay, do measure the willingness of intermediate recipients within government to pay on behalf of those ultimate recipients. With such revenue streams, conventional profit measures can be used by the providers of those services as though they were for-profits, including for the purposes of performance-related pay.

<table>
<tr><td>2.2</td><td>Challenges of performance measurement</td></tr>
</table>

2.2 Challenges of performance measurement

There are six serious challenges facing performance measurement in the definitive government case:

- measurement of costs
- reliability of output measures
- causal relationships between inputs and outputs
- narrowness of output measures
- comprehensiveness versus concision in reporting measures
- controllability of performance.

In performance measurement, costs must be measured using a full accrual basis – cash bases cannot measure the cost of the service provided. One challenge that governments share with for-profits and non-profits is that of distinguishing between the cases where full costs are required – typically perhaps in the financial reporting context – and those where full costs are not relevant – typically for short-term decisions. A particular challenge for governments is the typically large proportion of costs that are not naturally traced to outputs and outcomes, thereby involving significant amounts of arbitrarily allocated costs.

The second challenge is that of recording and communicating non-financial output measures reliably, which includes being capable of being audited. In comparison with accounting systems, databases of non-financial information are less reliable. Internal control systems for controlling money in to and out of the system are elaborate. Inputting non-financial information – especially in schools, hospitals, at crime scenes, battlefields – typically cannot be expected to be controlled to the same degree that money can. There are also likely to be few equivalents to the records of financial transactions that can be used to verify the data from these other situations. Also, there will never be the independent check of the numbers that is provided by bank reconciliation for the accounting systems.

The third challenge relates to causal relationships. The outputs and outcomes determined by the service professionals and politicians fundamentally affect the inputs that are the primary concern of accounting. The non-financial measures may be easy to count and should be reliably measured. Nevertheless, it is profoundly difficult for everyone involved to establish causal relationships between inputs, outputs and outcomes. This is even difficult when it is being done statistically, using large databases across organisations and programmes, in which mean performance, those above the mean and those below, and the outliers, are being identified. It is substantially more difficult when the performance is being measured once, for one organisation over one period. It might be thought that this would be easier, in that it more closely approximates laboratory conditions, but a government service is not a laboratory in which inputs, outputs and outcomes can be controlled by reducing it to discrete experiments, as important as any experiments that can be carried out may be. Dams cannot be built twice, to provide a control group, and students cannot be educated twice. Because the laboratories are not available, however sophisticated the analysis of performance, unintended consequences are the norm.

The fourth challenge relates to the nature of non-financial output measures: they are not comparable between services. The measurement is easy because it focuses on very specific characteristics. In Exhibits 2.1 and 2.3, the number of students is reliably measured but not all students are the same. The students in one secondary school are not the same as those in another, whether in the same city or not. For the same reasons, the teachers' and students' experiences in one year will not be the same as those of the previous year.

Introduce all the other services that a government might provide and it is clear that performance measurement primarily using non-financial output measures is necessarily diffuse. Comparisons cannot be made between numbers of students at secondary schools and primary schools even, but obviously cannot be made with numbers of clients of any other kind. The more specific the focus, the more useful the measurement. Measures that focus on complex, multiservice governments or on complex single services within a government will have to be very many. These will not be comparable and will not be capable of being understood in the context of a complex service or government as a whole.

The fifth challenge, then, is to determine a balance between the natural need to generate very many performance measures and the equally natural demand from service recipients, politicians and the population at large to be given a simple understanding of performance. Concise, partial performance measures can produce serious misunderstanding of the comprehensive performance of a government but a central imperative of those measures is for them to be understandable to non-specialists.

The sixth challenge relates to the controllability of government performance. In a rational control system, the performance measurement only relates to those matters that the government can control. The measures that are used are used throughout the planning, execution and monitoring cycle of the government. Accounting requires the measures to be systematically linked to costs and capable of being audited in some sense, so focuses on the measures to be included in the annual budget and in the audited financial statements. These measures are the only ones that are within the organisation's control.

Measurement itself is about simplifying the world. It is about reducing the complexities that we observe into simple objective components so that we can then deal with their essences with greater precision. Its extraordinary success in science and technology, notwithstanding the contestability at the margins, has not been repeated for settings in which people are inextricably involved, including organisations. In the medical sciences, we have been far more successful in dealing with people in physical terms than psychological terms. The rational approach to managing organisations always competes with, and can be dominated by, continually changing, grounded, ad hoc, trial-and-error approaches – that is, by muddling through.

There is general acceptance of the premise of performance measurement. That notwithstanding, it is important to understand any such system must be judged not only in the terms set by the system itself but also by the lived experience of those who provide and those who receive government services. We must at least allow that this could be very different from what the systems portray.

FURTHER READING

Atkinson, T. (2005) *Measurement of Government Output and Productivity for the National Accounts* (Atkinson Review: Final Report), Palgrave Macmillan.

Bouckaert, G. and Halligan, J. (2008) *Managing Performance: International Comparisons*, Routledge.

Boyne, G., Meier, K., O'Toole, L. and Walker, R. (eds) (2006) *Public Service Performance: Perspectives on Measurement and Management*, Cambridge University Press.

Kurunmäki, L. and Miller, P. (2006) 'Modernising government: the calculating self, hybrid-isation and performance measurement', *Financial Accountability and Management*, 22(1): 88–106.

Propper, C. and Wilson, D. (2003) 'The use and usefulness of performance measures in the public sector', *Oxford Review of Economic Policy*, 19(2): 250–67.

Shah, A. (ed.) (2007) *Performance Accountability and Combating Corruption*, World Bank.

Warburton, R. (2005) 'Preliminary outcomes and cost–benefit analysis of a community hospital emergency department screening and referral program for patients aged 75 or more', *International Journal of Health Care Quality Assurance*, 18(6/7): 474–84.

Chapter 3

Fundamentals of accounting

The technical fundamentals of accounting are the same in all organisations, whether governmental, for-profit or not-for-profit. The public sector context, however, shifts the emphasis among these fundamentals. Public sector accounting techniques require a return to accounting fundamentals to understand them. It is also important, because of the context, to understand that there are two other forms of 'accounting' that complement and sometimes compete with public sector accounting, especially in national governments. First, there is the set of macroeconomic accounts for each country (known as national accounting) and, second, there is each national government's budget.

3.1 Elements of accounting

Records of transactions – of each organisation – are the fundamentals of accounting, just as this aspect of accounting is fundamental to internal control. It is still common for governments to use forms of single-entry bookkeeping. In the Anglo-American context, single-entry systems are seen as archaic, belonging to the nineteenth century at the latest, but probably few double-entry systems are wholly comprehensive, integrated recording systems and the use of subsidiary systems (for accounts receivable, for example) is still common. The ever-increasing use of a few generic software packages will produce greater uniformity.

There is polarisation of views as to whether these records should be expressed in a uniform way across a set of organisations (the most basic elements of a 'chart of accounts') or left to each organisation to determine. Even in the latter case, at some level there is demand for some kind of uniform classification of the results of these transactions. The difference of opinion hinges on belief in the extent to which any accounting system can provide meaningfully uniform categories (of cost, for example). In extremis, a 'chart of accounts' believes that uniform records produce uniform categories; the polar view is that the economics of different organisations are different and no amount of uniformity in record-keeping can change that. In practice, there are very strong demands for some degree of uniformity – especially from politicians and non-financial managers – that have to be satisfied regardless of whether the underlying records are expressed in a uniform way or not.

Comprehensive, integrated double-entry recording systems can apply to each organisation taken as a whole, naturally producing one set of financial statements for each one. It is common practice, however, to keep sets of transactions (pools of resources) assigned to a particular purpose completely separate from other pools. The clearest form of this practice is in US state and local government accounting, in which these pools of resources are called 'funds' (so clear is it that the phrase 'fund accounting' has sometimes been used as shorthand for 'state and local government accounting'). These funds raise the basic question of whose transactions are being recorded by the organisation's accounting system: are they the records of the organisation or of a fund within it? The starkest example of this question might be where each fund also has its own bank account.

Although the question can raise complicated issues, the idea of a fund is simply a technical response to the instinct we all have to designate money to specific purposes, for a variety of reasons, sometimes because of the source of the money, sometimes because of our intended use. The idea is also common in business accounting, but the financial reporting imperative in Anglo-American accounting has long been seen to be the provision of one set of consolidated financial statements providing measures of revenues, expenses, assets, liabilities and cash flows for each organisation as a whole, which has tended to obscure important questions about the role of funds.

The enduring focus of accounting in government has been on the proper recording of these transactions. Closely associated with this has been control of spending against the budget.

Budgets are requests for, and subsequently authorisations to spend, public money and, at bottom, they are financed by taxation. The form of the requests is a plan for future spending, against which actual spending can be compared for internal control purposes and external control. Governments are publicly accountable during all stages in this control cycle, to varying degrees. In their definitive form, budgets are requests by the executive of a sovereign government for the authority from the legislature to collect taxes. In the context of local governments, they may be seen as requests by officers for the authority from the council of politicians; or the requests may be directly from the local government to the electorate, in the form of budget hearings.

Budgets may not be produced by accountants at all, but, once they have been approved, it is the role of accounting to monitor actual spending against the budget in order to provide a crucial form of control. As the form and content of the budget can significantly influence the extent of the control that is possible, accounting would always want a central role in forming the budget request. In the UK, at central and local levels, accounting has played just such a central role; in the USA and continental Europe, it is common for budgeting to be divorced from accounting.

Budgets developed as requests for money to spend, but in modern governments they are better described as requests to spend. This widens the nature of budgets from being only concerned with money as a medium of exchange to allowing other forms of spending (the definition of which depends on the basis of accounting) against the budget. Thus, spending can be defined as passing invoices for payment rather than the actual payment of cash.

These two definitions of spending have fundamental effects on budgetary control, which has particular emphasis on ensuring that budgets are not overspent. A system defined by cash payments provides natural limits to the amount spent (the cash available).

Another definition of spending that leads to a very different kind of budget is one that identifies the commitments (at the US federal level these are generally known as obligations; at the US state and local level, they are encumbrances) to spend as spending. Those commitments might be of different kinds (depending on the issue of orders to suppliers or the signing of contracts, including employment contracts), but they occur earlier, sometimes years earlier, than the processing of invoices for payment or their actual payment.

Control in a government is a means to an end, not the end itself. Governments exist to provide services; their recurring objective is to provide them better. The traditional role of accounting in modern government was limited to matters of financial probity, spending within budgets and the minimisation of spending. Matters relating to the quantity and quality of services provided were largely implicit and, anyway, were left to service professionals and politicians. During and since the second half of the twentieth century, however, there was a stream of initiatives, including budgeting initiatives, which shared the same fundamental premise: that, given scarce resources, explicit measurement of the quantity, if not the quality, of services provided, linked to measurement of resources consumed, produces better services.

The implementation of systems based on this premise requires the measurement of inputs and outputs, but it also requires the establishment of causal relationships between the measures of input, the low-level measures of outputs, the high-level measures of output and the unmeasured qualitative outcomes. This is of particular importance to accounting as, whatever else performance measurement systems achieve, they must relate outputs and outcomes to costs for them to have economic meaning. Moreover, any such systems must be judged not only in the terms set by those systems but also by the lived experience of government services, which we must at least allow could be very different from what the systems portray.

Knowing the causal relationships between measures of inputs and outputs is the foundation of for-profit accounting, significantly helped by the natural use of the same scale of measurement: money. Projected turnover drives the budgets, which then identifies the necessary production, which in turn identifies the costs that vary with output (sometimes called the engineered costs – the balance being termed discretionary costs). Cost–volume–profit analysis, with its attendant techniques of standard costing and variance analysis, is the underlying technique. It identifies that part of the cost structure in which costs do not vary with output – termed fixed costs; those that do vary but not continuously – the semi-fixed costs; and those that vary continuously – variable costs.

The proportion of engineered costs to discretionary costs varies by business and industry, the higher proportions being found in manufacturing, but, even in service industries in which causal relationships can be difficult to establish, the benefits of naturally occurring money measurement are available. The definitive cases in government, in which outputs can easily be measured but not in money terms, are also those in which most costs are discretionary.

There is an associated contrast between for-profit businesses and governments that identifies another fundamental difference in budgeting. The turnover that drives a business budget, in a profitable business, maintains the existing levels of equity and debt and can increase it in the form of retained earnings. In this sense, the profitable business can be said to be self-financing, in that the turnover finances the business. In a government, in this sense, it is the budget that finances, typically annually. Government budgets are recurring requests for finance, which, if not authorised, would result in the government ceasing to exist.

The form that budgets physically take varies across organisations, countries and over time, as does the form of all financial statements. Although budgets have not been subject to the attentions of standard-setting bodies in the way that financial reporting has, there are common features of budgets. Since the 1940s, these features have been challenged, particularly by the techniques of programme budgeting and zero-base budgeting, which were at the height of their popularity in the USA in the 1960s and 1970s. As comprehensive alternatives they failed to be accepted, but there are elements of each that continue to have relevance.

The traditional starting point of a budget is the organisational structure – or, more specifically, identification of those officers within the government who are held accountable for spending money against budgets. In the private sector, this would be known as responsibility accounting but, in fact, governments as a whole commonly structure everything – not just their finances – in terms of holding specific officials accountable for their actions, culminating in holding the government itself accountable. This feature of budgets applies whether budgets are held at a high level of aggregation or there is significant devolution of budgets: the organisational structure locates the budgets.

Within each of the budgets thus identified, there are other common elements. Budgets are usually listings of what is to be bought with the money being requested: they are lists of inputs. They may be very broadly specified and may, in extremis, be a single amount. They may also, and were more typically, specified in much detail. There might be one amount for the whole of the costs of employees, but this might also be broken down into very detailed items, such as overtime pay for wage-earners. Again, though, whatever the level of specification, budgets are usually lists of inputs. In the USA, accountants often label these as lists of 'line items', the same term being used in the financial statements.

The definitive budgets are for one year – the coming fiscal year. The form of this annual request embodies another common feature of budgets: the request for the coming year is justified in terms of the marginal changes made to the previous year's budget. When political scientist Aaron Wildavsky observed this part of government budgeting in the early 1960s, at the beginning of his celebrated work on budgetary processes, he called it 'incrementalism'. There was nothing new about the practice but his nomenclature has stuck, even though the word misleadingly implies that the practice must always lead to budgets increasing year on year. The essence of this feature of budgeting is not that budgets must always increase, but that they are justified by marginal changes from previous years, which may, in principle, be decrements.

Summing up these common features, their traditional form is of line item, incremental budgets that reflect the organisational structure. As they are expressed in money terms, they are natural ways to request money. They are also very good at providing a crucial sort of financial control that financial officers demand, in that the budgets specifically identify who is spending money and what they are buying with it. This demand is not only in the interests of the financial officers themselves but also that of the public, whose money is being spent. It is common in many countries for budgets to be enacted as law, in part to emphasise the importance of this kind of control.

In Europe in particular, in modern governments, the budget was used to impose central control on all aspects of governments. Rules were developed, many of which are still in use, to provide central control. Budgets that provide money for only a year, after which time they lapse, is one such (known as 'annuality'); another is the rule that budgets are provided gross, so that any income earned by a budgetholder must be surrendered to the central coffers (the 'gross budget principle'); the requirement that budgets balance (that budgeted spending is financed by taxation) was also common. This emphasis on central control was also associated – notwithstanding the fact that the size of government budgets since the late nineteenth century grew at unprecedented rates – with the idea that public money had to be spent on the cheapest that money could buy, especially for routine, recurrent spending.

It is important, in modern governments, to understand that annual budgets – as plans to spend money (however that spending is defined) – are not wholly discretionary. In practice, it is not possible to fix a budget anywhere between zero and the amount of last year's budget. Some spending takes place in governments whether an annual budget requests it or not, just as some taxes are collected whether the annual budget requests them or not. This is a pervasive practice, even though annual budgets are still thought of as being wholly subject to an annual cycle.

The reason is that earlier actions of the government, of different kinds, also determine spending and taxation. A law might have been passed that changes a payment to an individual from being subject to annual appropriation to an entitlement (unemployment benefit). Another might have been passed to determine the liability of an individual to pay tax when certain conditions are fulfilled. Line items are quantities of inputs acquired at various prices; the quantities may be judged fixed but the prices may change. A capital project might have been recently completed that now needs spending to operate it, if it is not to be mothballed. Depreciable assets depreciate as they are used, not as budget authority determines they will.

In principle, we presumably should allow that the worst case will force a government to liquidate part of its activities, perhaps even all, but these cases are not in the forefront of budgets in practice, in which some line items are under the control of the annual budget and some not. For the ones that are under that control, the budgets are targets, while for the ones that are not they are predictions. As targets, budgets are being used ingenuously to change the government's spending behaviour. As predictions, they are expected to be the best estimates of what the spending will be. In both cases, it is important to recognise that the budgets can be disingenuous for a wide variety of reasons.

The cycle of control that an accountant would want to see would begin with determining the budget, then continuous records of obligations made, invoices received and payments made. These records would then be compared with the budget to determine under- and overspending. In the traditional form of budgets, this is done at annual rests. At any such rest, the information available for net spending would be: actual 20x0, budget 20x1, estimated 20x1, budget 20x2.

The emphasis of public sector auditing has been, and still is, on propriety and probity, and on whether or not the transactions conformed to the budget. These financial and regularity audits now include the financial statement audit, which provides the auditor's opinion on whether the general purpose financial statements fairly present what they purport to present or not and whether or not they conform to the law related to financial statements. In the UK and the USA, financial and regularity audits depend heavily on internal control systems but are always separate from them. It is not uncommon in other governments, however, for auditors to be a part of such internal control.

In the traditional financial and regularity audits, judgements had to be made about the quality and quantity of services provided, but as these elements were not always measured, their part in auditing was tacit. This changed in the early 1970s with the publication by the US supreme auditor of the 'Yellow Book' of government auditing standards. This was the first codification of government audits and formalised the idea that government auditors must take a view on the quality and quantity of services provided in the light of resources consumed: performance auditing (also known as economy, efficiency and effectiveness auditing, and value for money auditing). Very often, however, the choice was made not to require auditors to offer opinions on the performance of governments, but, rather, require them to offer opinions on whether or not governments had installed suitable systems for allowing the governments themselves to judge their performance. In this way, audits stimulated an explosion of performance measurement, soon followed by explicit treatment of quality issues, although the governments themselves often developed the measures.

The most interesting and difficult issue in all of auditing is that of independence. In the private sector, this is a matter of the independence of auditor from auditee, as it is in many public sector contexts. In the context of sovereign governments, however, in which an audit is taken to be of the executive on behalf of the legislature, the independence of the auditor from the legislature is also relevant, to distance auditors from party political influence. In continental Europe, such auditors are, as a consequence, commonly part of the judiciary.

These elements of accounting and auditing are primarily concerned with the control that each governmental organisation, including a national government, has over its own affairs. Their natural focus is on financial control, being one part of overall control, but the way that it is exercised can vary. Modern governments were established by having central control of how money was spent (emphasis on the control of means). Subsequently, a competing view of control has developed that is a central control of the overall amount of money to be spent, accompanied by a control of what the spending achieves (emphasis on the control of ends), with the detailed control of means being devolved to the budgetholders. In practice, there will be mixes of these views of control, but the theme of centralised versus devolved control is a recurring one in budgeting, accounting and auditing.

3.2 Bases of accounting

The records of transactions of an organisation have to be comprehensive and accurate. The accounting bases of an organisation's budget and financial statements depend on when these transactions are recognised; which other revenues, expenses, assets and liabilities are recognised; and what measurement and valuation bases are then applied to all of the amounts so recognised. The accounting basis of the budget can be, and often is, different from that of the financial statements. The accounting basis of a government can be, and also often is, an amalgam of different bases for different line items – one comprehensive, internally consistent basis of accounting for a governmental organisation as a whole is unusual.

Exhibit 3.1 gives a summary of the transactions, and other data, for the City of Eutopia for a simple service provided by a depreciable asset (which refers mainly to assets and expenses not to liabilities or revenues), a minibus service operated by the Social Services Department.

Exhibit 3.1 Minibus Service, Social Services Department, City of Eutopia, for 20x2–20x5

At the beginning of 20x2, the department bought a minibus for £50,000, with a four-year life, and, at the end of 20x5, it had no scrap value. The minibus carried external clients for free. The annual cash payments for the vehicle service were £30,000 for the driver and £20,000 for the fuel and other vehicle expenses. All of these data are known, thus the example has no uncertainty in it and no changes in prices over the four years. There were no inventories at any of the year ends. The costs of buying the minibus and operating it were charged to the budget. The 20x2 annual budget for the minibus itself was £50,000, driver's costs £25,000 and fuel and other vehicle expenses £22,000. The budget for this service does not include the taxes and borrowing that implicitly finance it; these are under the control of the city as a whole.

The first stage in defining the accounting basis is to define when these transactions are recognised. For each transaction, there are three distinct points to consider (each point can be defined in practice in different ways, but the overall effects are the same). The latest of the three points is the cash payment to the supplier or employee (the practical differences in definition will relate to how cash is physically paid, whether by voucher, cheque or bank transfer, for example). This accounting basis is used by all organisations. It may be the only one used by a given government or it may be used in addition to many others. In Exhibit 3.2 the cash basis is used in the budgetary accounting.

Exhibit 3.2 Cash basis budgetary control report for the Minibus Service, Social Services Department, City of Eutopia, for first quarter 20x2

Minibus Service
Social Services Department, City of Eutopia
Budgetary Control Report
First quarter, 20x2

£	Annual budget	Cash payments to date	Under-(over-)spending against budget
[1]	[2]	[3]	[4]
Operating:			
Employees	25,000	7,500	17,500
Transport			
Fuel and other	22,000	2,000	20,000
Capital:			
Vehicles	50,000	50,000	0
Total	97,000	59,500	37,500

This shows that the actual operating cost cash payments by the end of the first quarter are significantly underspent when compared to the annual budget. This is of limited use for control purposes and, rather than comparing actual payments to the annual budget, it is more useful to look at the proportion of the budget expected to be used by the end of the first quarter. This is known as profiling. For the employee costs it might be expected that these would be paid out evenly throughout the year and therefore the profile would be £6250 (one quarter of £25,000). For the fuel and other costs, the expected cash payments by the end of the first quarter might, because of the normal delay in paying suppliers invoices, be only £2500, which is significantly less than one quarter of the annual budget. If the actual payments for the first quarter are now compared with the budgetary profile for the first quarter, this indicates an overspend of £1250 for employee costs and an underspend of £500 for fuel and other costs.

The second distinct point is the earliest one for each transaction: when the transaction is ordered from the supplier or employee. There are three names that can broadly be used for this point: commitment to spend (common in the UK); the encumbrance (common in US state and local government); and the obligation (used in the US federal government). The idea behind this distinct point is that, while control of the government depends on controlling cash payments, it also depends on controlling the transactions that the government commits itself to. This idea is particularly strong in budgetary accounting, where the focus is on using the budget to control what is spent against the budget. The cash payment is part of that control, but, if the government is already committed to making a given cash payment, even if it leads to a budget being overspent, the payment itself becomes a formality that cannot be varied. This has added emphasis given that an official order from a government to a supplier or employee, while it may not be a legal liability to accept the goods or services, can usually be taken by the supplier or employee to mean that the order will not be withdrawn or varied to their disadvantage.

This second distinct point can be applied in a government in two broad ways, which can be identified in this example by distinguishing between the transactions with the supplier and those with the employee. The commitment basis or encumbrance basis is typically used only for those line items that authorise large numbers of purchases made daily or weekly – in this example, for the fuel transactions with the supplier. The budgetary control it provides is primarily for the budgetholder's own purposes. The budgetholder needs the accounting system to keep a record of the initiation and completion of every transaction so that he or she continuously knows the amount of the budget not yet committed. The final accounting for the year against the annual budget is based on cash payments, so the budgetholder also needs to know the amount of the budget not yet paid out. Exhibit 3.3 gives a budgetary control report for the commitment and cash bases.

Exhibit 3.3 Commitment basis and cash basis budgetary control report for the Minibus Service, Social Services Department, City of Eutopia, for first quarter 20x2

Minibus Service Social Services Department, City of Eutopia Budgetary Control Report First quarter, 20x2					
£	Annual budget	Orders issued to date	Uncommitted balance of annual budget	Cash payments to date	Under-(over-) spending against budget
[1]	[2]	[3]	[4]	[5]	[6]
Transport					
Fuel	15,000	8,000	7,000	3,000	12,000

The two amounts of the uncommitted budget (Column 4) and of the cash balance for the budget (Column 6) are viewed differently by the budgetholder, even though his or her initiation of the transaction will lead to the payment for it. That is because of the segregation of duties in internal control – those who order goods and services do not make the payments for them. The budgetholder will actually issue orders, but the payments will be made by a payments office in the Finance Department, to reduce the risk that budgetholders will collude with suppliers in fraudulent or uneconomic transactions.

The crucial aspect of this segregation is that the budgetholder does not know when the payment will be made and therefore does not know when the budget will be charged with the payment. If the normal delay between the order issued and payment made for these kinds of purchases is a month or so, for most of the year the delay is not relevant in controlling spending for an annual budget as all orders issued in the year will lead to cash payments within the same year. Because of this, during the year it is the amount of the budget not yet committed that will be of most interest (Column 4), to ensure that the annual budget is not overcommitted. That means the need for a profile of expected cash payments by the end of the first quarter is less relevant here because the focus for control purposes is on the relationship between the annual budget, the commitments (the orders issued to date) and the uncommitted balance.

Towards the end of the year, the delay between an order and payment can mean that orders issued in one year lead to payments in the next. Therefore, towards the end of the year, the budgetholder's focus on Column 4 will be shared with actual payments to date (Columns 5 and 6). The focus on Column 4 during the year is because the budgetholder does not want to overspend against the annual budget; the focus on Column 6 is because the budgetholder does not want to underspend against it. The budgetholder's focus, then, while ensuring that the annual budget is not overspent, is on predicting how many orders can be issued to ensure that all the associated payments will be made by year end.

As a practical matter, because commitment systems most usefully relate to line items that authorise large numbers of purchases made often, the accounting can be complicated. There are many reasons for the financial amount of an order being different from the final payment. For example, the quantity and quality of goods delivered may not be what were ordered, prices may have changed, orders may be varied before delivery. The accounting basis, in practice, needs to be continually monitored to remain useful to the budgetholder.

The logic of commitment accounting follows from focusing on the earliest point of a given transaction, particularly a transaction with a supplier, but there is a second broad way in which that point can logically lead to a related accounting basis – the obligation basis. It can be identified in this example by focusing on all the transactions, including those with the employee. The budgetary control that the obligation basis provides is primarily for those who authorise the budget and for the top management who control the budget on their immediate behalf.

The annual budget authorises all the budgetholders to spend neither more nor less than the amounts authorised. The logic of the obligation basis is that, while control of the government depends on controlling all cash payments, it also depends on controlling all the transactions that the government commits itself to – or, we can say, obligates itself to. Every transaction must have an earlier point than the payment of cash. That is so even for transactions where the delay is very short, perhaps almost instantaneous, between deciding to buy and paying cash. It is also so for transactions such as salary payments to employees, in which the obligation is made when each contract of employment is signed. The obligation basis holds every budgetholder to account for not just paying cash but also obligating the government at earlier points to subsequently paying cash. Exhibit 3.4 shows a budgetary control report using the obligation and cash bases.

Exhibit 3.4 Obligation basis and cash basis budgetary control report for the Minibus Service, Social Services Department, City of Eutopia, for first quarter 20x2

£	Annual budget	Obligations to date	Unobligated balance of annual budget	Cash payments to date	Under-(over-) spending against budget
	Department A Budgetary Control Report				
	Month ended [date], 20x2				
[1]	[2]	[3]	[4]	[5]	[6]
Operating:					
Employees	25,000	7,500	17,500	7,500	17,500
Transport					
Fuel and other	22,000	10,000	12,000	2,000	20,000
Capital:					
Vehicles	50,000	50,000	0	50,000	0
Total	97,000	67,500	29,500	59,500	37,500

The exclusive use of the cash basis in a government restricts the budgetary control by that government as a whole to cash payments; all other aspects of control – including control of the obligations made by budgetholders on behalf of the government – are dealt with by the internal control system in other ways. Rules about the kinds of obligations, and the size of them, that can be entered into by a budgetholder without higher authorisation might be imposed in a variety of ways. Penalties for overspending cash budgets might be more severe, with explicit rules about how overspending is to be covered by other budgets within the year or beyond.

In contrast, the obligation basis, in conjunction with the cash basis, adds to the budgetary control itself the control of the obligations made by budgetholders on behalf of the government. In its extreme form, the obligation basis states that any obligations entered into by a budgetholder for which there is no remaining – unobligated – budget for the year are void. Orders issued to suppliers are cancelled, however much the supplier may already have done to satisfy an order. The orders cannot be applied to next year's budget because that budget, even if it has already been passed, only authorises obligations to be made in that subsequent year, not in the current year.

A fundamental problem that the obligation basis can have is best identified by comparing it with the commitment basis. The logic of the two bases is the same. The application of the logic is clearest under commitment accounting because all of the transactions it is applied to clearly begin with an official order that results in an associated cash payment. The recognition by the accounting basis of the earlier point of each transaction is clear and frequent. This clarity and frequency only applies to a small proportion of government budgets, however.

Most budgets are dominated by salaries, for which that earlier point is clear (the signing of each employment contract), but the point at which each decision is made not to terminate the contract or not to vary it is usually not frequent. For the obligation basis to be applied comprehensively, artificial points have to be imposed. For example, the total annual salaries payment is said to be obligated at the beginning of the year or, more likely, the monthly salaries payment is said to be obligated at the beginning of each month or else perhaps at the point during the month that the actual payment is certain. None of these points has any significance for the politicians who authorised the budget. The obligation basis in such cases becomes a formal one with no practical effect.

The obligation basis, with the cash basis, can distinguish between operating payments and capital payments, as in Exhibit 3.4 but otherwise operating and capital are accounted for in the same way. The budget authorises the full amount of each transaction, whether operating or capital, in terms of both the obligation to pay and the payment itself. The most unusual and significant aspect of this is that the budget scores the full amount of a capital project at the time of the obligation.

This is of great significance for the internal control of budgetholders, but also for the external control of the government as a whole. Under this basis, the politicians who ultimately adopt a budget are being forced to count all capital projects, for their full amount, at the time of the budget. How that budget is to be financed – particularly the proportions to be financed by taxation and borrowing – will mitigate the effects of this. When borrowing is allowed for capital projects (explicitly or implicitly), the politicians can immediately glean the benefits, in voters' eyes, of authorising capital projects while using borrowing to postpone the costs to taxpayers. At least the budget does immediately score the full amount for the capital projects. A balanced budget on the obligation basis, defined to prohibit borrowing, would additionally force the taxpayers to pay that full amount immediately.

The earliest and latest points when transactions might be recognised by accounting are the commitment/obligation and the cash payment. The third possible accounting basis lies between these two points: the accrual of the transaction – when the goods or services were delivered and an invoice issued. This point does not apply to many transactions in government budgets. The salaries line item is again a good example of transactions that are often large parts of budgets for which the cash payments are the only significant accounting basis as they are typically neither subject to 'orders' nor to invoices. For those line items that do relate to goods and services bought on credit, however, the accrual basis is of very great significance. The cash basis is always and everywhere necessary. The commitment basis and the obligation basis can be very relevant, but they cannot record the cost of using the goods and services bought on credit. Only the accrual basis of the transactions can do that as it is the only basis that is comprehensively defined by the possibility of using the goods and services.

The accounting bases of transactions have been illustrated so far in budgetary control. The accrual basis can be similarly illustrated, but budgets are, in practice, likely to be cash-based, with or without the commitment or obligation basis. The accrual basis is, therefore, more likely to be restricted to the financial statements. Once we have illustrated the accrual basis in the context of the financial statements, we can return to its implications for budgeting.

The accrual basis of transactions provides only the foundation for accrual accounting. What also needs to be defined is which other revenues, expenses, assets and liabilities are recognised and what measurement and valuation bases are then applied to all of the amounts so recognised. The term 'accrual accounting' is authoritatively used to refer to different definitions of all these aspects. Even when the term is used (implicitly or explicitly) to mean comprehensive accrual accounting, the definitions vary. It is useful, therefore, to refer to each of these not as 'the full accrual accounting basis' but 'a full accrual accounting basis'. Of equal significance, in government accounting, there are many variations in the use of partial accrual accounting bases – indeed, they are probably the norm. In some contexts, they are referred to as 'the modified cash basis' or 'the modified accrual basis' – the usefulness of both terms being that they identify a basis that is somewhere between a pure cash basis and a full accrual basis. The variety of detail underpinning these generalisations, again, suggests that it is more useful to refer to each of them as 'a modified accrual basis'.

Exhibit 3.5 provides a full accrual accounting example using the Minibus Service, with additional data.

Exhibit 3.5 Full accrual basis financial statements for the Minibus Service, Social Services Department, City of Eutopia, for 20x2–20x5

At the beginning of 20x2, the department bought a minibus for £50,000, financed by an earmarked loan for four years, repayable at the end of each year in equal instalments, at 3 per cent interest. The minibus had a four-year life and, at the end of 20x5, it had no scrap value; the depreciation policy is straight-line. The minibus carried external clients for a fee, set so as to break even for the service – a financial objective that the service did achieve each year. The annual cash payments, and the accrued expenses, for the vehicle service were £30,000 for the driver and £20,000 for fuel and other vehicle expenses. There were no inventories at any of the year ends. There was no working capital at any of the year ends; fees collected provided any necessary working capital within the years. All of these data are known, thus the example has no uncertainty in it and no changing prices over the four years.

Exhibit 3.6 provides the operating statement and balance sheet for the data in Exhibit 3.5.

Exhibit 3.6 Full accrual basis financial statements for the Minibus Service, Social Services Department, City of Eutopia, for years ended [date], 20x2–20x5

	Minibus Service Social Services Department, City of Eutopia Years ended [date], 20x2–20x5			
£	20x2	20x3	20x4	20x5
[1]	[2]	[3]	[4]	[5]
Operating statement				
Operating revenues				
Fees	64,000	63,625	63,250	62,875
Operating expenses				
Employees	30,000	30,000	30,000	30,000
Transport				
Fuel and other	20,000	20,000	20,000	20,000
Depreciation	12,500	12,500	12,500	12,500
Finance costs:				
Interest on debt	1,500	1,125	750	375
Total expenses	64,000	63,625	63,250	62,875
Net surplus (deficit) for the year	0	0	0	0
Statement of financial position				
ASSETS				
Non-current assets				
Vehicles	37,500	25,000	12,500	0
LIABILITIES				
Current liabilities				
Current portion of long-term borrowing	12,500	12,500	12,500	0
Non-current liabilities				
Long-term borrowing	25,000	12,500	0	0
TOTAL NET ASSETS	0	0	0	0
NET ASSETS				
Capital contributed by the government	0	0	0	0
Accumulated surpluses (deficits)	0	0	0	0
TOTAL NET ASSETS	0	0	0	0

In this example, the cash basis and the accrual basis for the transactions is the same (because there are no receivables or payables or inventory at the end of the year). In practice, the difference between the two bases for transactions may or may not be materially different to a government's financial statements. The essential difference between the two bases in this example, as often in practice, is that the full accrual accounting recognises an additional expense – depreciation.

There are two fundamental points about the depreciation charge. First, it transforms the cash-based total costs of the service shown in Exhibit 3.4 from £97,000, of which £47,000 are operating costs and £50,000 capital costs, into a measure of the economic cost of the service provided in the year (usually shortened to 'cost of service provided'), by excluding unallocated costs of the vehicle and including a measure of the costs of the vehicle used up by operating it.

Second, it offers the possibility of using the financial statements to report on capital maintenance. By abstracting from price change, both the financial concept of capital and operating (or physical) concept of capital are demonstrated. The example assumes that no capital was invested in the service (it having been financed by borrowing) and shows that the full accrual accounting adopted maintained that capital at the end of every period at zero. This second point is used as a basis for judgements of the fairness of the service in charging fees to the clients. Each year's clients pay the same amount of the costs over the four years (a simple contribution to the very complex issue of intergenerational equity).

Exhibit 3.7 develops the Minibus Service to illustrate one of the many forms that a modified accrual accounting might take.

Exhibit 3.7 Modified accrual basis financial statements for the Minibus Service, Social Services Department, City of Eutopia, for 20x2–20x5

At the beginning of 20x2, the department bought a minibus for £50,000, financed by an earmarked loan for four years, repayable at the end of each year in equal instalments, at 3 per cent interest. The minibus had a four-year life and, at the end of 20x5, it had no scrap value; the depreciation policy was straight-line. The minibus carried external clients for free, financed by taxation. The city applies its balanced budget constraint to the service, requiring taxes to be raised each year to cover total costs. The annual cash payments, and the accrued expenses, for the vehicle service were £30,000 for the driver and £20,000 for fuel and other vehicle expenses. There were no inventories at any of the year ends. All of these data are known, thus the example has no uncertainty in it and no changing prices over the four years.

Such accounting might decide that the operating costs of the driver, fuel and so on should be on an accrual basis, so that the financial statements give the cost of the service provided for those line items. In this example, there is, once again, no numerical difference between the cash and accrual basis (because of lack of closing payables/receivables and inventories). The city might not want to charge the service for depreciation, however, which would be required by full accrual accounting. On the other hand, it might want to charge the service for the principal repayments of loans, which would not be required by a full accrual accounting (repayments of loans being balance sheet movements on a full accrual basis). Exhibit 3.8 would be the resulting financial statements for this modified accrual basis.

The total annual cost of the service is not different from the full accrual basis shown in Exhibit 3.6, but the accounting basis is. That is because the full accrual basis measures the cost of service provided, while the modified accrual basis does not. This fundamental difference could lead to very different annual costs. In Exhibit 3.7, change the assumption that the vehicle was financed by borrowing to one that the vehicle was donated, as it may well be in a Social Services setting. The annual cost would drop by the exclusion of the principal repayments of loans and the interest. The two costs under the modified accrual basis adopted would be very different, but neither would measure the cost of the service provided.

It is true that the Exhibit 3.7 example demonstrates how a modified accrual basis can be used to maintain capital intact as, if the vehicle was financed by a

Exhibit 3.8 Modified accrual basis financial statements for the Minibus Service, Social Services Department, City of Eutopia, for years ended [*date*] 20x2–20x5

Minibus Service
Social Services Department, City of Eutopia
Years ended [*date*], 20x2–20x5

£	20x2	20x3	20x4	20x5
[1]	[2]	[3]	[4]	[5]
Operating statement				
Operating revenues				
Taxes	64,000	63,625	63,250	62,875
Operating expenses				
Employees	30,000	30,000	30,000	30,000
Transport				
Fuel and other	20,000	20,000	20,000	20,000
Finance costs				
Interest on debt	1,500	1,125	750	375
Principal repayments	12,500	12,500	12,500	12,500
Total expenses	64,000	63,625	63,250	62,875
Net surplus (deficit) for the year	0	0	0	0
Statement of financial position				
ASSETS				
Non-current assets				
Vehicles	37,500	25,000	12,500	0
LIABILITIES				
Current liabilities				
Current portion of long-term borrowing	12,500	12,500	12,500	0
Non-current liabilities				
Long-term borrowing	25,000	12,500	0	0
TOTAL NET ASSETS	0	0	0	0
NET ASSETS				
Capital contributed by the government	0	0	0	0
Accumulated surpluses (deficits)	0	0	0	0
TOTAL NET ASSETS	0	0	0	0

loan (or, for that matter, by a donation), the capital would still be shown as zero at each year end. The assumption that each year's taxpayers were paying a fair share would hold. That is the essence of this modified basis: it forces the service, and the politicians who are ultimately responsible for it, to raise taxes each year to pay for capital assets, even though borrowing is allowed. A strict balanced budget requirement would forbid borrowing and force them to bear the whole of the costs of the capital assets when they were incurred. The usual reason for relaxing this requirement is that it would not be fair to the taxpayers in the year in which the capital asset was bought, given that future years' clients will benefit from the asset and/or the taxpayers would be unwilling to pay. The modified accrual basis illustrated here provides a middle way between the strict balanced budget and the wholly unbalanced budget that might be applied under Exhibits 3.2 and 3.4, depending on the way that the city finances its overall budget.

The full accrual basis shown in Exhibits 3.5 and 3.6 can be developed by applying different measurement and valuation bases in two main ways. First, the example can address specific and general price change and, second, the example can include a charge for the opportunity cost of capital.

In Exhibit 3.6, the value of the vehicle in the balance sheets is historical cost net of depreciation, which gives the possibility of calculating an operating concept of capital maintenance in addition to the financial concept in nominal money terms. To address specific price change, in Exhibit 3.9 one price change has been added – namely that the replacement cost of the vehicle increased to £60,000 at the end of 20x2. The revaluation has been made in Exhibit 3.10, with an adjustment to the annual depreciation charges. The operating concept of capital views it not as money but as the services provided by the vehicle itself. At the end of 20x5, when the vehicle must be replaced for the service to continue, it can be done with the same level of borrowing as at 20x2, using the accumulated reserves. Under the operating concept, the reserves are capital adjustments. Under the financial concept, where capital is zero throughout the four years, the reserves (held in cash and resulting from the recovery of the replacement cost increase, from charges) are not capital: they can be used for any purpose, operating or capital.

Exhibit 3.9 Full accrual basis financial statements with revaluation, for the Minibus Service, Social Services Deaprtment, City of Eutopia, for 20x2–20x5

At the beginning of 20x2, the department bought a minibus for £50,000, financed by an earmarked loan for four years, repayable at the end of each year in equal instalments, at 3 per cent interest. The minibus had a four-year life and, at the end of 20x5, it had no scrap value; the depreciation policy was straight-line. The minibus carried external clients for a fee, set so as to break even for the service – a financial objective that the service did achieve each year. The annual cash payments, and the accrued expenses, for the vehicle service were £30,000 for the driver and £20,000 for fuel and other vehicle expenses. There were no inventories at any of the year ends. There was no working capital at any of the year ends; fees collected provided any necessary working capital within the years. All of these data are known, thus the example has no uncertainty in it. There are no changing prices over the four years, except that the replacement cost of the minibus at the end of 20x2 was £60,000.

The change in valuation basis from Exhibits 3.6 and 3.10 fundamentally changes the measure of the cost of service provided in each of these full accrual bases and, in this example, fundamentally change the charges made to the year's clients. Which of the two costs of the service provided is the better one is a matter of opinion. In this example, the essence of the difference lies in whether the clients in 20x6 and beyond should pay the full amount for the vehicle that they will use (in which case borrowing would have to be £60,000 at the beginning of 20x6) or they, in each of the years from 20x2 to 20x5, should pay the economic cost (market price) of using such a vehicle in each of those years.

To address general changes in prices, in Exhibit 3.9 a general price increase of about 5 per cent a year for the years 20x2 to 20x5 could be added, meaning that the general purchasing power of the currency in 20x5 was about 20 per cent less

Exhibit 3.10 **Full accrual basis financial statements with revaluation, for the Minibus Service, Social Services Department, City of Eutopia, for years ended [*date*] 20x2–20x5**

Minibus service			
Social Services Department, City of Eutopia			
Years ended [*date*], 20x2–20x5			
£	*20x2*	*20x3*	*20x4*	*20x5*
[1]	[2]	[3]	[4]	[5]
Operating statement				
Operating revenues				
Fees	66,500	66,125	65,750	65,375
Operating expenses				
Employees	30,000	30,000	30,000	30,000
Transport				
Fuel and other	20,000	20,000	20,000	20,000
Depreciation	15,000	15,000	15,000	15,000
Finance costs:				
Interest on debt	1,500	1,125	750	375
Total expenses	66,500	66,125	65,750	65,375
Net surplus (deficit) for the year	0	0	0	0
Statement of financial position				
ASSETS				
Current assets				
Cash and cash equivalents	2,500	5,000	7,500	10,000
Non-current assets				
Vehicles	45,000	30,000	15,000	0
LIABILITIES				
Current liabilities				
Current portion of long-term borrowing	12,500	12,500	12,500	0
Non-current liabilities				
Long-term borrowing	25,000	12,500	0	0
TOTAL NET ASSETS	2,500	5,000	7,500	10,000
NET ASSETS				
Capital contributed by the government	0	0	0	0
Reserves	2,500	5,000	7,500	10,000
Accumulated surpluses (deficits)	0	0	0	0
TOTAL NET ASSETS	2,500	5,000	7,500	10,000

than it was in 20x2. This would not affect the operating concept of capital, but it would affect a financial concept of capital, in that it might suggest maintaining financial capital during a period of general price increase would lead to a real reduction in financial capital. If the financial concept of capital were to be calculated in real terms, an additional sum of about £2500 would have to be charged over each of the four years to maintain financial capital at zero in 20x5 units of currency (5 per cent of £50,000 to maintain the purchasing power of £50,000, which is £60,000 in 20x5 units of currency). Without this charge, capital in 20x5 measured in 20x2 units of currency would be negative.

The second way to develop the full accrual bases in Exhibits 3.9 and 3.10 is to add a charge for the opportunity cost of capital. Such a charge is not made in for-profit accounting under either the International Accounting Standards Board's or the Financial Accounting Standards Board's standards as the cost of debt is an expense, but the cost of equity is not recognised. The economic argument for charging the opportunity cost of capital is that the opportunity cost of both debt and equity capital is a part of the cost of the service provided. The accounting problem in applying this argument in financial statements is that the cost of capital cannot always be reliably measured. When this charge is made – as it is with the UK central government's full accrual basis – the percentage is arbitrarily determined and imposed on all financial statements. In Exhibit 3.10, the charge would be applied to the opening net book value of each line item, so that a 5 per cent charge for the vehicle would produce additional charges to the operating expense of £3000, £2250, £1500 and £750 respectively in the years 20x2 to 20x5 – that is 5 per cent of the opening book value of £60,000 for 20x2, 5 per cent of opening book value of £45,000 for 20x3 and so on). As, however, the net assets of the service are mainly offset by borrowing and the total net assets therefore small, the overall charge for the opportunity cost of capital would be close to zero.

The full accrual accounting bases illustrated in Exhibits 3.6 and 3.10 are restricted to the financial statements. If, however, these bases were judged to be the most relevant bases for the financial statements, a complete cycle of control would require that the budgetary accounting, and indeed the budgets, should adopt the same basis. Accrual budgeting would be a radical change for most government accounting. It was added to the UK central government's budgets for each government department on adoption of a full accrual accounting but as an addition to cash-based budgeting, not as a substitute. Exhibit 3.11 provides an annual accrual-based budgetary account using the accrual basis of Exhibit 3.10, which can be compared with the obligation- and cash-based budgetary account for the annual budget shown in Exhibits 3.1 and 3.4.

Exhibit 3.11 Accrual-based budgetary account for the Minibus Service, Social Services Department, City of Eutopia, for the year ended [*date*] 20x2, using the accrual basis of Exhibit 3.10

£	Original budget	Actual	Difference between original budget and actual: under (over)
OPERATING BUDGET			
Employees	25,000	30,000	(5,000)
Transport			
Fuel and other	22,000	20,000	2,000
Depreciation	12,500	15,000	(2,500)
TOTAL OPERATING BUDGET	59,500	65,000	(5,500)
CAPITAL BUDGET			
Vehicles	50,000	50,000	0
TOTAL CAPITAL BUDGET	50,000	50,000	0

Minibus Service
Social Services Department, City of Eutopia
Comparison of Budget to Actual
Year ended [*date*], 20x2

The main point of Exhibit 3.11 relates to the treatment of the cost of the minibus itself. In accrual budgetary accounting, capital is strictly distinguished from operating expense, using the financial statements' definition of what is and what is not capital. The capital costs are then put in a separate, capital budget. The link between the capital budget and the operating budget is the depreciation charge – an operating expense. Exhibit 3.11 includes the effects of the revaluation of the minibus at the end of 20x2. This revaluation did not affect the capital budget, as it would not affect the obligation- and cash-based annual budget: the minibus was budgeted to cost £50,000, that amount was obligated and then paid. The revaluation did affect the accrual-based operating budget, though, as the depreciation budget was based on the cost of the minibus at the time of budgeting, but the accrual-based financial statements restate that depreciation cost to recover the replacement cost at the end of 20x2.

This point illustrates an important disagreement between those who support obligation-based budgeting and those who support accrual-based budgeting. The central argument of obligation-based budgeting is that the cost of capital projects is scored in full in the budget at the time the decision is made to authorise the budget for the project. This is seen as important in controlling the politicians who authorise the budget. It is then contrasted with the way that accrual-based budgeting scores the capital costs over the life of the assets (through the depreciation charge) in the operating budget.

The counter-argument is that accrual-based budgeting also scores the full amount in the capital budget at the time of the decision. In practice, this counter-argument can have less force because of the different ways that a separate operating budget and a separate capital budget might be financed. If the government decided that the capital budget could be financed by borrowing, while the operating budget had to be financed by taxation, then, from the politicians' point of view, the scoring against the capital budget hurts much less than it does when it is against the operating budget. Thus, the obligation-based budget is a single (unitary) budget that scores all costs – operating and capital – at the time they are obligated.

Accrual-based budgeting might respond to this argument by insisting that the capital budget can be controlled to the same degree as the operating budget, but perhaps in different ways. Part of this could be to not concede that the capital budget can be financed by borrowing, but accrual-based budgeting would also shift the focus of the argument.

Obligation-based budgeting exclusively scores transactions, from obligation to cash payment. It is predicated on the long-standing provision (in the US federal case there is even a constitutional provision) that government money cannot be spent without the authority of the legislature. Accrual-based budgeting would point out that spending money is not the only way of incurring costs. In this example, depreciation of depreciable assets occurs whether the legislature authorises it or not, merely as a result of using the assets. The more general points are that obligation- and cash-based budgeting cannot budget for the cost of services to be provided by the government and does not necessarily include asset or liability recognition or changes in them that are other than cash-based.

A particularly troubling characteristic of cash bases is the ease with which the underlying transactions can be manipulated. Any accounting depends on the integrity of the transactions. The consequent records and the subsequent measurement and valuation that produce relevant reports have to be reliable. The cash basis has no exogenous way of defining when cash should flow, either in or out. The amounts that should flow can be defined but not when. Given the centrality of the fiscal year in accounting, this lack of definition means that the annual account can be seriously manipulated, without in any way being judged improper – beyond commonsense judgements. Cash payments can be properly postponed by as little as 24 hours to yield markedly different operating statements and balance sheets. For example, the monthly salaries bill can, with the agreement of the employees, be postponed from the end of month 12 in the old fiscal year to the beginning of month 1 in the new. An accrual basis appeals to the measurement of the cost of services provided to identify that there would then only be 11 monthly salaries payments in the old year and adjusts for that fact; a cash basis has nothing to which to appeal.

3.3 National accounting and government budgeting

There are two other forms of 'accounting' that complement and sometimes compete with public sector accounting, especially in national governments. The first is the set of macroeconomic accounts for each country (known as national accounting) and, second, there is each national government's budget.

National accounting is a statistical system that produces economic statistics for each economy, particularly of national income and wealth. As well as the focus on each economy, it focuses on each of five sectors within the economy: two for business (finance and non-finance), one for non-profits, one for households and one for government. The operating statements and balance sheets for the last of these – known as the general government sector – provide a competing view of a national government from that provided by government accounting as a whole.

National accounting is a globally standardised system that derives its theoretical framework from economics and is carried out by central statistical offices. In its modern form, it developed from the 1930s onwards, as part of the macroeconomic management that had emerged in the USA and the UK to deal with the Depression. World War II then provided a special impetus. Governments in the UK and then the USA had the responsibility of deciding which resources should be applied to the overriding military needs (and export need) and which to the civilian population.

To do this systematically and rationally also required knowledge of the nation's available resources. The national income accounting that developed subsequently promoted and reinforced the peacetime national economic perspective that the UK increasingly adopted, accompanied by a surge in the nationalisation of utilities and other fundamental services. National income accounting became known as national accounting as the theory and practice added balance sheets to the operating statements. The global system is called the System of National Accounts, with a European version that is fully consistent with the global system. Another set of national economic statistics that developed in parallel – known as the Government Finance Statistics – focuses on economic relations between economies.

National accounting has much in common with accounting. Both use money for their measurements; national accounting is accrual-based and government accounting includes accrual bases; national accounting depends, in part, on the accounting records of transactions in each organisation; and national accounting partially defines itself in terms of its points of departure from for-profit accounting.

National accounting, however, is also very distinctly different from accounting (as a matter of language, obviously confusingly so), even though both systems are in part addressing the same economic activities of government. National accounting uses a 'double-entry' system, but it is fundamentally different from double-entry bookkeeping.

The two versions of 'double-entry' have a common foundation – a transaction is recorded as an exchange between two parties, in which each party is taken to benefit equally. Double-entry bookkeeping, however, keeps the records of actual transactions of a single organisation, but national accounting records aggregate estimates of actual transactions between five large sectors, which are groupings of organisations (and people).

There are two obvious consequences of this different definition of a 'transaction'. The first is that the transactions of double-entry bookkeeping can be audited in the narrowest and most traditional sense of that word: they can be verified as correct. The transactions of national accounting, however, cannot be audited in that sense. The second is that double-entry bookkeeping provides the possibility of external verification of a balancing figure: the amount of cash at the bank. The double-entry in national accounting cannot provide such a check.

Other fundamental differences between national accounting and accounting are that the reporting entities of national accounting are the aggregate sectors of the economy, not individual organisations, and the definition of the general government sector is not necessarily a government's definition of itself or an accountant's definition of it. Moreover, the definition of accruals for particular line items can be very different, in theory and practice. One striking example is accounting's requirement for inventory to be an asset, contrasted with national accounting's requirement for it to be an expense.

National accounting, then, by its nature, demands comparable information across each economy. In countries such as the UK and the USA, accounting – also by its nature – cannot provide such information. National accounting avoids this contradiction essentially by using statistical processes. It has produced, in a single country, significantly different income figures for gross domestic product measured from different points of view. This is an obvious weakness, but it does produce relevant data in standardised forms worldwide.

Both national accounting and government accounting provide inputs to a national government's budget, but each budget's rules and practices are typically distinctly different. They are not, and cannot be, apolitical, being at the heart of government. The rules are developed by each government, which protects its sovereignty over those rules. They are subject to the due process of law and practice, but those processes can be arcane, ad hoc, complicated – and far from

transparent. There are international pressures on the rules and practices (from bodies such as the International Monetary Fund, World Bank, OECD), but there is no international set of policies. Government budgets can, therefore, draw on an array of accounting bases, legitimated within accounting or national accounting, as well as by the assertion of sovereignty, to produce an amalgam that has no technical meaning.

FURTHER READING

Aiken, M. (1994) 'Parliamentary sovereignty and valuation accruals: uncongenial conventions', *Financial Accountability and Management*, 10(1): 17–32.

Anessi-Pessina, E., Nasi, G. and Steccolini, I. (2008) 'Accounting reforms: determinants of local governments' choices', *Financial Accountability and Management*, 24(3): 321–42.

Caperchione, E. and Mussari, R. (2000) *Comparative Issues in Local Government Accounting*, Kluwer.

Christiaens, J. and Rommel, J. (2008) 'Accounting reforms: determinants of local governments' choices', *Financial Accountability and Management*, 24(1): 59–75.

Ellwood, S. (2008) 'Accounting for public hospitals: a case study of modified GAAP', *Abacus*, 44(4): 399–422.

Jones, R. (2000) 'National accounting, government budgeting and the accounting discipline', *Financial Accountability and Management*, 16(2): 101–16.

Lüder, K. and Jones, R. (eds) (2003) *Reforming Governmental Accounting and Budgeting in Europe*, Frankfurt: Fachverlag Moderne Wirtschaft.

Mellett, H. (1997) 'The role of resource accounting in the UK government's quest for "better accounting"', *Financial Accountability and Management*, 27(2): 157–68.

Perrin, J. (1998) 'From cash to accruals in 25 years', *Financial Accountability and Management*, 18(2): 7–10.

Van der Hoek, M. (2005) 'From cash to accrual budgeting and accounting in the public sector: the Dutch experience', *Public Budgeting and Finance*, Spring: 32–45.

Chapter 4

Budgetary policies and processes

Budgets are at the heart of government. They are requests for – and, subsequently, authorisations to spend – public money. At bottom, they are financed by taxation. The form of the requests is a plan for future spending, against which actual spending can be compared for internal control purposes and external control.

4.1 The rational control cycle

Governments exist to provide services and their recurring objective is to provide them better in the future. The rational approach to deciding what services to provide, including the quantifiable risks and non-quantifiable uncertainties of the future, is sequentially to make analytic plans in advance, implement them, compare actual results against the plans and use the experience gained to improve future plans. These actions together form the sequential planning, execution and monitoring cycle.

The rational approach is required for major technical projects that are complex and capital-intensive. For the remaining bulk of government services, common sense suggests that this approach is more useful when there is less uncertainty, in the physical world (including its climate) and in the people involved. During periods of great uncertainty, the only experience gained might have been that the plans had been useless, even to the point of threatening the survival of the organisation. Moreover, however successful our understanding of the physical world is, our understanding of people's behaviour, individually and in groups (and in different cultures), is very far from complete. Indeed, it can even be argued to be primitive. The rational approach to managing organisations always competes with, and can be dominated by, continually changing (and often) grounded, ad hoc, trial-and-error approaches – that is, by muddling through.

The rational approach to control is applied by different groups for different things. Departments apply it to their primary focus, so, a social services department applies it to social services in that government, while a central support department such as human resources applies it to personnel. Governing bodies as a whole, in conjunction with its senior officers, apply it to the government as a whole or to services that are clearly provided by more than one department, perhaps involving other organisations, in partnership or otherwise, such as in a transport plan. Although the rational approach can take many different forms, there are common elements that can usefully be identified.

It is natural, in thinking about the future, to plan for the long-, medium- and short-term (say, more than five years, one to five years, one year), reflecting greater to lesser degrees of uncertainty. Similarly, and perhaps consequently, plans can vary from being broadly expressed to including great detail. They can also vary from being largely qualitative to largely quantitative.

Medium- to long-term plans focusing primarily on outcomes, broadly expressed, largely qualitative but containing key quantities, non-financial and financial are often referred to as strategic plans (containing strategies), especially when developed mainly by officers. When they are discussed in the context of politics, however, they are more generally referred to as policy documents (containing policies). It is common to distinguish strategies (or policies) from operational plans (tactical or logistical plans, when the military origins of the word are favoured), which are short- to medium-term, expressed in more detail, with greater use of quantities, including of financial amounts. The more quantitative the plans, the more use can be made of economic or financial modelling.

In strategic and operational plans, the planned outcomes can variously be called aims, goals, missions, objectives, purposes, targets. Of these, 'missions', 'aims' and 'purposes' tend to be used in the broader, qualitative senses; 'goals', 'objectives' and 'targets' in the narrower, quantitative ones.

A chronic problem with strategic and operational plans in all organisations is the link – typically the absence of links – between them. While they can rationally be distinguished, and identifying the individual aspects of each can be useful, a five-year, qualitative mission that bears no relation to current financial resources will probably not be worth stating.

Budgeting is one of the rational tools of control, its special importance deriving from the fact that its main focus is on money. It has the same function in governmental, not-for-profit and for-profit contexts. Government budgets begin as requests for money, all or part of which become authorisations (sometimes formally called appropriations) to spend money, and, at bottom, they are financed by taxation. As money pervades government activity, budgets can dominate other forms of control. Once budgets have been authorised, allocating scarce resources to competing claims on those resources, spending departments spend against them. Thus, control can be exercised in relation to these budgets (during and after the spending). The period of the budget that dominates is for one year.

Full accountability would require all stages in the budgetary cycle to be publicly transparent and, indeed, as no one would doubt that financial reporting should be audited, all other stages should be subject to audits in some form. In for-profit and many not-for-profit organisations, the details of plans (including budgets) are often taken to be confidential to each organisation. Governments, on the other hand, are publicly accountable at all stages in this cycle (though not always to the same degree). As it happens, the interest of politicians and the public in this cycle is overwhelmingly weighted towards the authorisation of the budget and away from the financial statements produced after the spending. The interest of the spenders might tend in the same direction, though spenders naturally have incentives also to be concerned about control. For accountants, however, the emphasis is primarily on control.

Budgets are not always produced by accountants but, once they have been authorised, it is the role of accounting to monitor actual performance against the budget: to provide a crucial form of control. This is mainly financial control but, particularly when budgets include output measures, this can be a wider form of control. Detailed elements of this financial control by the budget are:

- determining budgeted expenditure and income (with special emphasis when a strict definition of a balanced budget is imposed)
- setting a standard for evaluating financial performance
- motivating budgetholders
- coordinating the finances of the government as whole, with added emphasis in multipurpose governments.

Also, as the form and content of the budget can significantly influence the extent of the financial control that is possible, accounting would always want a central role in forming the budget request. In the UK for example, at central and local levels, accounting has played such a central role; in the USA, in marked contrast, some governments divorce budgeting from accounting.

A recurring theme in budgeting is that the non-financial control and financial control functions of budgets can conflict. The primary focus of the organisation is naturally on outcomes, on the services that governments provide. The financial control focus shifts to money – to where the money comes from and what it procures. The rational approach to control precisely links these, but a focus on outcomes can produce a form of budget that is unsuited to financial control, because what the government is ultimately trying to achieve may not be reflected by the organisational structure. Thus, a focus on inputs can produce a form of budget that is unsuited to control of outputs even, much less of outcomes.

In modern governments, annual budgets – as plans to spend money – are not wholly discretionary. In practice, it is not possible to fix a budget anywhere between zero and the amount of last year's budget. Some spending takes place whether an annual budget requests it or not, just as some taxes are collected whether the annual budget requests them or not. This is pervasive practice, even though annual budgets are still thought of as being wholly subject to an annual cycle.

The reason is that earlier actions of the government, of different kinds, also determine spending and taxation. A law might have been passed that changes a payment to an individual from being subject to annual appropriation to an entitlement (unemployment benefit). Another might have been passed to determine the liability of an individual to pay tax when certain conditions are fulfilled. A law might have been passed imposing on a department or on a lower-level government the duty to provide a service, defined in specific input, output or outcome terms. Line items are quantities of inputs acquired at various prices. Although the quantities may be judged fixed, the prices may change, which is outside the control of the government. A capital project might have been recently completed that now needs to be operated, requiring money to be spent if it is not to be mothballed. Depreciable assets depreciate as they are used, not as budget authorities determine that they will depreciate. Debt issued by a government, on unspecified security, has to be financed with contractual interest payments, and redemption, on due dates. Employment contracts constrain the government significantly, given that employees typically consume a large percentage of budgets. Decreases in operating spending, by eliminating jobs, say, may not be achievable in the short run and may anyway be more than offset by increases in one-off payments to compensate employees for the loss of their jobs.

In principle, we presumably should allow that the worst case will force a government to liquidate part of its activities, perhaps even all of them, but these cases are not typical of budgets in practice. More typical are budgets in which some line items are under the control of the annual budget and some not. For the ones that are under that control, the budgets are targets, while, for the ones that are not under that control, they are predictions. As targets, budgets are being used ingenuously to change the government's spending behaviour. As predictions, they are expected to be the best estimates of what spending will be. In both cases, it is important to recognise that the budgets can be disingenuous, subject to gaming. Budgets are crucial to all politicians and spending departments, but they address the uncertain future, the outputs and outcomes of budgets are contestable; they are ripe for subjective evaluation and political bargaining, including among the controllers and the controlled.

Who authorises budgets depends on the context, and the differing contexts can significantly influence the budgetary policies and processes. In their definitive form, in sovereign governments (in which there is naturally a legislature), budgets are requests from the executive to the legislature, which subsequently authorises. The use of the word 'budget' derives from the eighteenth-century British government context and was coined from the French word '*bougette*', meaning a small purse. In modern governments, there can be a role for auditors, separate from the executive and the legislature, given that budgets to some extent depend on assumptions about the future that can, in some sense, be audited. Once the legislature authorises the budget, the executive is then able to spend it. Detailed control is usually a matter for the same executive (Finance Ministry, Treasury), but ultimate accountability to the legislature will be exercised in the form of financial statements of actual spending. The specific nature of this control is in part defined by the form of the budgets.

In these sovereign governments, the budgets may be authorised by law and, for their departments and agencies, will be. The control cycle in such cases is, at its highest level, carried out by legislators, using the law. In some governments, this form of control dominates; in others, it is more a matter of ritual, with the executive exercising the detailed control. A fundamental characteristic of this relationship between the legislature and executive is that governments are complex, as is their accounting, but legislators generally do not have the incentives and, as legislators, do not have the technical expertise to understand these complexities.

In governments below the sovereign level, budgets are authorised differently. In cases such as local governments, in which there are directly elected politicians who run the local government in some form of council, the paid officials produce the budget requests (perhaps coordinated by the chief financial officer) and the council authorises the budget. This authorisation may have been accompanied, even determined, by the electorate directly in budget hearings. Detailed control is then exercised by the paid officials, with ultimate accountability to the council. In governmental organisations in which there are no directly elected politicians, the governing body may provide the authorisation of budgets, but this may also be within, perhaps even related directly to, the authorisation of a higher-level governmental body.

Budgets are necessary because resources are constrained. It is the accountant's, sometimes the economist's, task to identify – before or at the time of budget authorisation at the latest – where the resources are coming from to finance the budget. These resources may be grants, donations and so on, but, in the definitive case, the key decision is about the mix of borrowing and taxation. Broadly, this decision is known as balancing the budget, but there are specific definitions of balanced budgets that governments can, or are forced to, adopt, which have profound effects on control. A strict definition of a balanced budget is that it is financed wholly by taxation, with no borrowing (a loose definition is it is financed largely by borrowing). A budget financed wholly by taxation is strict in commonsense terms (whether the common sense relates to each of us as individuals or to organisations): the coming year's services are to be paid for by the coming year's taxpayers. This is only one of many controls, but it is one that all can understand. Whether a government can afford to spend what its budget authorises it to spend is, in the definitive case, a matter of whether or not it can collect the necessary taxes. For a narrow but enduring sense of control, the sooner it can collect those taxes, the better.

In discussing differing definitions of balanced budgets, it is important to note that there are special characteristics of the budgets of sovereign governments, and particularly of national governments, that influence the discussion significantly. A national government can usefully be thought of as an organisation (though it is important in theory and practice to remember that national governments are very complex sets of departments, agencies and so on) with its budget being a budget for that governmental organisation, as a request and authorisation to spend so as to provide that government's services.

A national government's budget is much more than this, however. It is also a budget for the economy as a whole and even, in some sense (because national budgets are used for wider purposes than economics) for the country – and perhaps beyond. A pivotal moment in modern government, when this expanded role for a national government's budget became clear, occurred in 1933, in peacetime but during major economic depression. In the USA, the federal government explicitly, and President Roosevelt specifically, produced a budget that included a substantial increase in spending to be financed not by taxation but by borrowing. Before and after this, J. M. Keynes had argued that the UK government should have done, and should do, the same. Both the US practice and Keynes' theory confronted the orthodoxy that governments should not borrow to finance their budgets in peacetime (in the knowledge that during wars, which had always appeared – as they still do – borrowing to pay for them could not be avoided).

This orthodoxy is generally referred to as the need for governments to authorise balanced budgets – broadly meaning that the annual net spending (net of miscellaneous income) should be financed by taxation. The essence of the challenge was that, while the orthodoxy was sound for a national government's budget taken in isolation, it was unsound for economies as a whole when they were severely depressed. In such cases, national governments should temporarily use their unique power to borrow to stimulate for-profit activity by individuals, families and businesses by providing grants, loans and tax relief, as well as invest in infrastructure. Once the necessary economic wealth has been created, the national government's budget can return to the orthodoxy of balanced budgets, releasing available borrowing for direct investment in the private sector.

In this view, the budget is still seen in terms of rational control, but it is controlling the economy, not just the government. Local governments do see themselves as having parallel roles in their localities or regions, but their powers are significantly fewer. In a national government, crucial elements of the budget can be directly influenced, sometimes determined, by the government itself. The level of interest rates, the quantity of money and general price change (fundamental elements of monetary policy) are obvious examples. In certain circumstances, these may be given exogenously by markets and, anyway, are typically under the formal control of central banks. National governments, however, have significantly more influence on these factors than a local government, whose budgeting task only focuses on predicting what these levels will be during the financial year and what effects they will have on that local government's spending and financing.

In conjunction with the national government's monetary policy, its fiscal policy (meaning its own spending and financing) is expressed in terms of the economy as a whole. A balanced budget is defined not in terms of the relationship between the national government's own spending and financing, but in relation to the rest of the economy. When the annual budget does not balance, the deficit to be financed by borrowing is justified in relation to the economy as a whole. Thus, a deficit would commonly be expressed, and justified, as a percentage of national income (say, gross domestic product), as would the government's accumulated debt.

By definition now, the national government's budget potentially affects everyone in the economy and, for a national government that is big enough, perhaps many in the rest of the world. All government budgets within the country, including lower-level governments and governmental agencies, will be directly affected by this budget. Its foundations are not matters of accounting. Economics and statistics measure national income and wealth, including the particular contributions that individuals, families, businesses and governmental bodies make to them. Rules of thumb about acceptable levels of debt are not matters of accounting.

Judged in rational control terms, national budgets necessarily make heroic assumptions about the ability of any group of people to plan and control the behaviour of millions of individuals', groups' and organisations' activities in a country, much less in regions and major parts of the world. At our current levels of understanding, this kind of control is impossible at the limit, perhaps even well within the limits, but it is of great importance and government budgets, at all levels, depend on it.

Budgets 'cascade' throughout the public sector (and the private sector). In the UK in particular, they often 'start' from the centre of government, in which case budgetary controls can be observed 'from above'. At all other levels, though, there are often two views of those controls. One looks upwards to the source of the budget and one looks downwards to where the budget is delegated. Thus, budgetholders in spending departments, whatever rules their budgets are subject to, might disaggregate those budgets further and impose different rules on subordinates. Another important feature of the cascade is that spending a budget can be viewed as having taken place once a budget is passed to another entity, either within the public or private sectors.

Perhaps the most important part of the cascade, which may not be best reflected in the choice of metaphor, is the complexity of budgets (and therefore the complexity of any principles of budgeting). In the UK the budget's unitary status implies an interlocking of all government budgets, as well as a relationship between these budgets and the finances of many private sector organisations, not-for-profit and for-profit alike.

4.2 Fiscal years

In their traditional form, and still in their most fundamental form, budgets authorise spending for one year. As this is not necessarily the calendar year, it has its own term: the fiscal year (relating to the public fisc, which is a largely obsolete term for public money) or, more generally, the financial or accounting year. This annual cycle is typical for organisations of all kinds, but, in governments, it often has special aspects to it and, as such, has its own word: annuality.

In its extreme form, annuality means that once the financial year ends, all authorisations to spend money against that budget end and all financial elements of contracts the government has signed lapse, including employment contracts. Hence, for example, in the absence of a budget for the subsequent financial year, government officials are sent home, without pay, and contractors have to renegotiate their contracts with the government.

At the other extreme, the annual budget is closer to a guide that does not directly have legal consequences and may not have formal consequences at all. However annuality functions in a particular government, the core of the control cycle is an annual one. Despite the obvious problems with the domination of annual cycles, we all still expect – and get – annual budgets and accounting. There are ways of attempting to address these problems, some more successful than others, but annuality persists.

At its highest level, the control cycle is managed by politicians on behalf of the public (taxpayers and/or voters), whose money it is that is being spent, but their accountability, at an election, is rarely annual. The multiyear terms of office between elections do not necessarily coincide with sets of financial years. There is a logic that would suggest the ideal planning and control cycle for the public would be one in which the politicians at an election include a budget for their prospective term of office in their manifestos, which the voters then authorise by virtue of their votes, and against which the voters control actual spending. The many practical obstacles, not the least of which is the information asymmetry between the incumbent politicians and those in opposition, usually prevent the implementation of this logic, but it is an important part of understanding why budgets deviate from the rational ideal.

Another problem is that the management cycle of particular services is not necessarily the same as the fiscal year. In education services, for example, the academic year is often different from it. This is perhaps nothing more than a technical problem for the budgetholders and controllers, but it is one that can have practical difficulties, such as when new appointments are made at the beginning of an academic year, but the consequences of next year's annual budget are not recognised.

A further problem is that many government activities take longer than a year to materialise. Major capital projects (which accounting usually defines as physical projects giving benefit over more than year), such as offices, airports, roads, hospitals, schools and so on, commonly take more than one year to construct. Major programmes, such as literacy or economic development, take many years for their benefits to emerge. In other words, in stable governments, one year is the short term and decisions have to be made in the contexts of the medium- and long-term. Trading-off the present and the future is fundamental to our lives and politics, economics and accounting, but the dominance of the annual budget can militate against such rational trade-offs.

While one year may be the short-term in stable settings, in uncertain contexts it can be too long. The authorised annual budget can be rendered irrelevant by changes in circumstances long before the subsequent budget is passed. The instability can be so severe as to suggest that a budget should be capable of being continually changed, and often – perhaps even to the point of being effectively continuously changed.

The process of preparing an annual budget request and obtaining its authorisation in any complex organisation can take so long before the financial year begins that, no sooner has the budget been approved, than the process begins again for the subsequent year's budget. Spending officers and accountants tend to feel that they spend the whole year budgeting. This problem suggests that a budget covering a period longer than a year would be useful. The most natural response to this argument would be for budgets to cover two or three financial years rather than fractions of financial years.

When the budget is based on the fiscal year, as it usually is, the form of the annual budget, or some variant of it, is as shown in Exhibit 4.1. In it, the budget for 20x2 is based on the budget for 20x1. At the time of producing the budget (just before the fiscal year 20x2 begins), much of the 20x1 budget has been executed. The government therefore has more knowledge of how the 20x1 budget will turn out and so a revised 20x1 budget can be produced, which should help to determine the 20x2 budget. The only actuals that are available at the time of budgeting for 20x2 are those for 20x0.

Exhibit 4.1 Annual budget column headings for the City of Eutopia, for fiscal year 20x2

	City of Eutopia Budget Year ended [date], 20x2			
£000	Actual 20x0	Original budget 20x1	Revised budget 20x1	Budget 20x2

In addition to the annual budget, the government may produce a medium-term budget, also based on fiscal years. Exhibit 4.2 is an obvious form for the future years' budgets.

Exhibit 4.2 Medium-term budget column headings for the City of Eutopia, for fiscal years 20x2–20x5

	City of Eutopia Budget Years ended [date]			
£000	Budget 20x2	Budget 20x3	Budget 20x4	Budget 20x5

4.3 Budgeting for inputs, outputs and outcomes

Performance measurement requires the planning, execution and monitoring of the government's service provision to include measurement of specific services. The consequent non-financial measures are not, in themselves, necessary for the financial control of a budget. The traditional forms of budgetary control of inputs can be separated from the service provider's control of outputs and outcomes, and typically were. That was not just because of technical difficulties with non-financial measures but also because service providers use their expertise about outputs and outcomes as arguments for overspending (and sometimes – though less often – underspending), thereby attempting to undermine budgetary control.

The separation of inputs from outputs and outcomes is not rational, however. The rational approach to control links them. Explicit consideration, including measurement, of outputs and outcomes is demanded by politicians, taxpayers and service users, so the task for the accountant is to link them with budgets. For all the reasons that performance measurement is very challenging, this task is also very challenging. The traditional measures of cost per head (student, client, patient) and cost per thousand of the population link input and output and are useful, but they are very crude proxies for outcomes and are not the kinds of performance measures used by politicians, taxpayers or service users. The kinds of direct output measures that are so used have to be simple and very specific, so are unsuited to representing the complexities of planning, execution and monitoring of service provision. The typical resolution of this dilemma is for budgets to be accompanied by a few output measures of incremental change in performance, only therefore implying causality between inputs, outputs and outcomes rather than asserting it.

4.4 Budgetary processes

The process of budget preparation and authorisation is long and complex, and itself can consume significant resources. It is described in a written set of budget instructions so that every participant is aware of what is required, but the informal negotiations and bargaining can never be completely captured by a written code.

In the definitive case, the process produces an authorised budget just before the fiscal year begins. The reason for aiming as close to the fiscal year as possible is to minimise the inevitable uncertainties in predicting a year ahead, as well as to have as much information about actual spending in the current year as possible. The reason for aiming for authorisation before the fiscal year begins is obvious, especially in systems in which spending of any kind cannot take place until a budget has been authorised. It can be a delicate balance, between not too late and not too early, but, even so, the process that leads to striking the balance is typically long.

The process in a particular government will vary, but, in general, there are three distinct stages. The first stage involves the preparation of budgets for each individual budgetholder in the government. These are then combined to enable the overall position to be considered. It is often necessary to revise the individual budgets at this stage before the draft budget for the whole can be prepared. In the final stage, the draft budget is submitted to the governing body for final approval. This could include a distinct intermediate step in which the budget, or parts of it, are presented to voters for comment or even for approval if participatory budgeting is practised.

Whichever part of the government is responsible for these stages will have considerable power in that government. Turning the needs and desires of individual budgetholders within a government into those of the government as a whole is emphatically not neutral. Even when resources are plentiful, there are always competing demands to spend them. Given the importance of budgets to financial control, the accountants in a central finance department would want to be responsible for the detailed preparation of the budgets of the various service departments or geographical divisions, with the service departments or geographical divisions only providing necessary information. Even when the service departments and geographical divisions would do all the detailed work, a finance department would normally still be responsible for keeping, if not making, the uniform rules, setting timetables, giving guidance on assumptions about economic and financial conditions and providing specialist financial information (on debt and support service costs, for example), as well as summarising the overall budget.

A crucial question for any budgetary process is whether it is to begin with the determination, by the governing body, of an overall limit on spending for the fiscal year. Such a limit can be expressed in a number of common ways:

- as a percentage increase – in nominal, cash terms – over the current year's budget
- as a percentage increase in real terms – an increase that exceeds the percentage of general price change
- as a percentage cut – in nominal or real terms – in the current year's spending.

The polar alternative is for the governing body to begin by asking budgetholders to produce budgets of what their needs and desires are. As budgeting is defined by limits on spending, an overall limit will emerge at some point in the process, but it could do so during the second or final stages.

Beginning the budgetary process with overall limits on spending affects the fundamental nature of the authorised budget. Even budgets that have only the barest reference to outputs and outcomes are embodiments of the needs (and desires) of budgetholders and resources. In complex governments, it is not possible for the governing body to know in advance of the fiscal year what the budgetholders' needs are (even if they want to). Therefore, overall spending limits cannot refer to needs, only to resources. Given that, what can the rational basis of an overall spending limit be, if the prices of inputs will change between the setting of the limit (months in advance of the fiscal year), the authorisation of the budget (just in advance of the fiscal year) and the spending during the year?

One rational basis for the limit could be to not set it in nominal, cash terms but in real terms. In other words, the limit is set by guaranteeing that individual budgets (and, therefore, the overall budget) will be automatically adjusted for the effects of any price changes between the beginning of the budgetary process and the final spending in the fiscal year. Such a system of indexation of budgets has been called volume budgeting ('volume' referring to the quantities of inputs rather than their prices) and is especially attractive during periods of significant inflation.

Such indexation, if it is to be completely rational, should relate to specific price changes, rather than general price changes. Specific prices are the prices for specific goods and services; general prices are statistics (indexes) of baskets of specific prices, of which there are many possible combinations, each defined by the particular goods and services to be included at the particular quantities; relative prices are the differences between a specific good or service and a general price index. Specific prices are the prices that budgetholders have to pay, recorded in their line items.

In practice, though – and not least because of the size and complexity of governments – volume budgeting tends to become the general price level indexation – the institutionalisation of inflation. When this happens, the principle behind volume budgeting is obscured because, in the absence of synchronised inflation (in which all specific prices increase by the same percentage), the quantities authorised in the original budget are not maintained. Another practical problem is that, in order to keep the price-level adjustments to the budget under control while prices are changing rapidly during a year, the budgets have to be anchored, as it were, in prices of a particular point in time rather than the prices actually paid during the fiscal year. Under volume budgeting, budgets are of 'funny money' (in the same way that historical cost operating statements and balance sheets with current purchasing power adjustments are).

In contrast to volume budgeting, overall spending limits set in advance of the budgetary process can be said to deny quantity as budgets are set as amounts of cash (sometimes called cash limits) with no explicit or implicit quantity of goods or services to be bought with them. They might be accompanied by a general assumption about prices (often set at a deliberately low level by a national government to dampen inflationary expectations in the economy), but, once the limit has been set, it is assumed it will not change before the budget is spent.

Budgetary processes that begin with overall spending limits will have line items that are excluded from the limits, if only because of those line items that are 'demand-led' because the law (other than the budget law, when applicable) has established entitlement to government money when certain criteria are met (as with unemployment benefit). This puts budgetary control at the mercy of claimants.

A particular challenge for the setting of overall spending limits is whether or not to apply the same limits to all budgetholders. For example, when resources are suddenly, obviously going to be limited, the government could impose equal across-the-board cuts. Other options might be to impose complete 'recruitment freezes' or adopt a last-in-first-out approach to cost reductions – that is, cut the most recently commenced services or programmes. In hard times, such cuts can be perceived as 'fair', but, when faced with the prospect of long-term organisational decline, the rational response might be to adopt strategies that will minimise the impact on fundamental aims and objectives. The problem for a budgetary process that begins with an overall spending limit is the limit itself does not allow this rational response because it has no basis for the harder choices. The political expediency of across-the-board cuts can create more chances for political conflict.

A budget prepared by a budgetholder under an overall spending limit is of a different nature from one produced under volume budgeting. Under a limit, even when prices are not significantly changing, the governing body is explicitly denying a level of quantity of goods and services and therefore implicitly denying a level of outputs and outcomes, leaving those problems to the budgetholders. In extreme forms, such overall limits can be interpreted as the centralisation of power and decentralisation of responsibility. However implausible the general price level assumptions made in the limits are, it is the budgetholder a number of stages removed from the centre of government who has to resolve any contradictions. This effect is further exacerbated by the use of formula funding for distributing cash to budgetholders, especially using formulae that are deliberately crude, often based on head counts. Under 'devolved management', the manager then has the responsibility of managing and being accountable for a wide range of financial and non-financial targets. The way that such budgets are prepared and used might be expected to be different or, at least, it would not be surprising if they were.

FURTHER READING

Berry, A., Coad, A., Harris, E., Otley, D. and Stringer, C. (2009) 'Emerging themes in management control: a review of recent literature', *British Accounting Review*, 41: 2–20.

Faulkner, D. and Campbell, A. (eds) (2006) *The Oxford Handbook of Strategy*, Oxford University Press.

Gilmour, J. and Lewis, D. (2006) 'Does performance budgeting work? An examination of the Office of Management and Budget's PART Scores', *Public Administration Review*, September/October: 742–52.

Joyce, P. (2008) 'Does more (or even better) information lead to better budgeting?', *Journal of Policy Analysis and Management*, 27(4): 945–75.

Kelly, J. (2005) 'A century of public budgeting reform', *Administration and Society*, 37(1), March, 80–109.

Pendlebury, M. and Jones, R. (1985) 'Governmental budgeting as ex ante financial accounting', *Journal of Accounting and Public Policy*, 4(4): 301–16.

Posner, P. (2007) 'The continuity of change: public budgeting and finance reforms over 70 years', *Public Administration Review*, November/December: 1018–29.

Posner, P. (2009) 'Budgeting process reform: waiting for Godot', *Public Administration Review*, March/April: 233–44.

Sterck, M. (2007) 'The impact of performance budgeting on the role of the legislature: a four-country study', *International Review of Administrative Sciences*, 73(2): 189–203.

White, J. (2009) 'What not to ask of budget processes: lessons from George W. Bush's years', *Public Administration Review*, March/April: 224–32.

Wildavsky, A. (1975) *Budgeting: A Comparative Theory of Budgetary Processes*, Boston: Little, Brown.

Wildavsky, A. (1984) *The Politics of the Budgetary Process* (4th edn), Boston, Little, Brown.

Chapter 5

Form and content of budgets

The forms that budgets of each governmental organisation physically take, and their associated content, vary across organisations, countries and over time. Accounting standard-setting bodies have significantly increased the uniformity of operating statements and balance sheets, but the same pressures have not been applied to the same extent to budgets. Nevertheless, there are common forms that can be identified.

5.1 Organisational and programme structures

Each organisation produces a budget for the organisation as a whole. How that budget can be structured in detail varies. If the organisation has a hierarchical structure, in which the government is a hierarchy of specific officials accountable for their actions, culminating in holding the top officials and politicians accountable for the whole, the most natural form for the budget is that organisational structure. The other side of this accountability is that the organisational structure reflects the power structure in the organisation, so the associated budget does, too. Hierarchical structures remain the commonest form of governments, the specific officials typically being grouped in ministries or departments.

Within a given organisational structure, the budgets can be held at a high level or they can be significantly devolved. The organisational structure still locates the budgets, but the way in which the organisation is managed will be different: managing a department with a budget fundamentally changes the scope of the management possibilities from managing a department without a budget.

Departments in the typical hierarchical case are groups of service specialists who, by virtue of their training and certification, have specific responsibilities relating to their specialism and may even, when they are certified by a private sector professional body, have formal responsibilities to that professional body and the public at large beyond their responsibilities to their governmental employer. Such specialisms can be characterised, for example, as military or civilian; within the military as army, navy, air force; as civilians as teachers, police officers, fire officers, refuse collection and disposal officers, social workers, traffic engineers, recreation officers, librarians, cemetery officers, engineers; as corporate support services as planners, lawyers, human resource officers, marketers, information and communication technologies (ICT) officers, as well as finance officers. The hierarchical structure requires all of these groups, ultimately, to be part of the accountability of the organisation as a whole, but it also requires them to manage as specialists.

The accounting system, being based on records of transactions, covers the organisation as a whole and down to the smallest details. How records are aggregated and reported will, in a rational organisation, match the budgets, such that budgetholders are in control of the net spending for which they are held responsible.

Budgets based on hierarchical organisational structures dominate government budgeting. Exhibit 5.1 provides a basic form for such a budget.

In our example, Corporate Services consists of the central support departments, such as Planning, Legal, Human Resources, Marketing, ICT, Estates Management and Finance. The departments listed that directly deliver the government's services are a small selection of the typical ones. The budgeted and actual figures for these departments are given as net expenditure, on the basis that any revenues that each department is responsible for collecting will be included within that department's budget. The budget is for the government as a whole so it also includes revenues that are projected to finance the government as a whole.

Exhibit 5.1 **Annual budget for the City of Eutopia, for fiscal year 20x2, based on the organisational structure**

£000	City of Eutopia Budget Year ended [date], 20x2			
	Actual 20x0	Original budget 20x1	Revised budget 20x1	Budget 20x2
Net expenditure				
Corporate Services	7,050	6,500	6,750	7,500
Education Department	20,500	22,000	23,500	25,000
Police Department	15,110	18,000	17,200	20,000
Social Services Department	12,250	13,000	12,900	14,500
Transport Department	5,030	6,000	6,400	6,900
Total net expenditure	59,940	65,500	66,750	73,900
Government revenues				
Taxes	30,460	35,000	28,880	37,900
Grants	24,570	28,000	29,000	33,000
Donations	2,350	2,500	2,100	3,000
Total government revenues	57,380	65,500	59,980	73,900
Total government net expenditure	2,560	–	6,770	–

The bottom line in the budget gives the surplus or deficit to be financed by borrowing. A strict balanced budget requirement would require it to be zero (or negative if revenues were to exceed expenditure) for 20x2 (and the same would have been required for 20x1). A cash basis for budgetary accounting could include the projected borrowing within the government revenues, in which case the bottom line would give the surplus or deficit for the year.

The organisational structure is the necessary form for the budget in the control cycle, but other forms can be useful. A common supplementary form is a programme structure, which has to be created in addition to the organisational structure. A programme structure is a written statement of the objectives of the government, representing the low-level and high-level outputs and outcomes that it wants to achieve from the services it provides. It shifts the focus of the budget from how the government is organised to provide services to what those services want to achieve, a shift from inputs to outcomes, with an emphasis on outputs when measurability is required. The programme structure is an enduring part of what was the otherwise unsuccessful comprehensive budgeting technique known as programme budgeting.

For many governmental organisations, the organisational structure is different from the programme structure. This is especially true in multipurpose governments where the programme structure cuts across departmental boundaries. A national government's programme on the illegal supply and use of drugs could include many different departments and agencies (diplomatic, military, customs, police, social services, education), with different and sometimes competing ways of carrying the programme out – from military operations in foreign countries, focusing on supply, through to primary school education, focusing on demand. In single-purpose governmental organisations, it is less true (by definition), but even in such cases the programme structure provides a different view from that of the entity as a set of organisational units. It must also be remembered that, although the focus of this discussion is on budgets for organisations, the logic of programmes includes the possibility that programmes usefully cut across organisations as well, even if that possibility brings even greater complexity.

Take the example of a police department, which provides a service that has strong technical elements but also wide social impacts. Programmes that are primarily the responsibility of that department are therefore likely to involve other departments of government. For example, the detection of crime might be separated from the prevention of crime. Within prevention of crime, the programme might emphasise police activities focusing on deterring, say, young homeless people from committing crime. A complementary, or even competing, alternative, however, might involve Social Services Department activities focusing on finding jobs and homes for those young homeless people, with the help of Economic Development Department activities to create the jobs and homes. All three departments would be supported by the Corporate Services departments, part of the activities of which would therefore also focus on the prevention of homeless youth crime. Such programmes clearly cut across departmental boundaries and so a programme budget reflects this.

Given that a programme budget supplements the one based on the organisational structure, a reconciliation is made to retain the integrity of each form of the budget. Exhibit 5.2 is an example of a crosswalk between the two forms, based on an extract from Exhibit 5.1.

Exhibit 5.2 **Crosswalk between the organisational structure and a programme budget for the City of Eutopia, for fiscal year 20x2 (extract)**

| £000 | City of Eutopia Budget Year ended [date], 20x2 | | | | |
	Programme A	Programme B	Programme C	General (unallocated)	Total
Net expenditure					
Corporate Services	1,000	1,000	500	5,000	7,500
Education Department	18,000	3,000	2,000	2,000	25,000
Police Department	500	500	17,000	2,000	20,000
Social Services Department	3,000	5,000	500	6,000	14,500
Transport Department	500	500	500	5,400	6,900
Total net expenditure	23,000	10,000	20,500	20,400	73,900

There is a technical accounting problem that arises from having these two budgets. It exists with any budget, but it is significantly greater with two. The problem is one of cost allocation. Organisational structures always include a set of costs – in this example for Corporate Services. These central support services are joint costs that cannot naturally be traced to each department, so accountants develop arbitrary, but useful, methods for allocating them.

In programme budgets, the allocation problem is much greater as the costs of employees and land and buildings, in all spending departments and in Corporate

Services, must be allocated to each programme. The amount of arbitrary allocation that must be done, as a matter of mathematics, increases. Whether this becomes a serious problem or not can only be judged in each practical case. Perhaps the employees, if not their places of work, can naturally be thought of as belonging to organisational units and programmes, but perhaps they cannot. The size of the equivalent final column to the one in Exhibit 5.2 represents the size of the problem in each case.

These different views, reflected in documents as pervasive as budgets, can be profoundly different ways of thinking about government services. The organisational structure is itself a power structure and can be taken as a given, in this context. A programme structure can, however, subvert that in different ways. An important set of ways of doing this involves representing the organisation not in the way that it exercises its power but in the way that people receive the services it provides. The more the focus shifts to the service receiver, the more radical the questions about how the services could be better provided.

Gender budgeting has provided a good example of thinking about the form of the budget in a different way. It is predicated on the idea that gender is an important variable in helping to explain human behaviour and, therefore, budgets should acknowledge and respond to gender difference. In Exhibit 5.2, hypothesised female factors could be substituted for the Programme columns to show a different view of the budget than that provided by the organisational structure. For example, it might be hypothesised, and empirical support might be found, that a factor such as 'feeling secure' is significantly different for men than for women. Organisational budgets for most government services might then be expressed differently, highlighting how much of those budgets was being spent on making women feel secure in that specific female sense, rather than assuming, as budgets often do, that 'feeling secure' is gender neutral.

5.2 Capital budgets

Capital, in this sense, means spending that provides tangible benefits to the organisation over more than one year. It often relates to complex infrastructure projects. Capital spending can be included in the annual budget in the same way that operating spending is, but such projects do not naturally fit into an annual cycle. That is not only because their tangible benefits extend beyond, sometimes well beyond, one year but also because they often take more than one year to move from being authorised to being available for operations. There are thus advantages to separating the capital budget from the annual operating budget and then reconciling the two budgets. A capital budget can be produced each year, but there are also circumstances in which it is renewed every few, perhaps even five, years.

The two kinds of budgets can also have different financing implications. Because capital projects provide tangible benefits over more than one year, there is a natural sense in which it is proper to finance them by borrowing, thereby perhaps matching the benefits for each year's taxpayers with the costs by spreading them. This is a difficult issue, even though it has a strong element of common sense, and anyway could be irrelevant in the context of a government that has decided on the need for fiscal stimulus. More importantly, however, any financing implications are separate from the usefulness of capital budgets as control documents.

Because capital projects are often technically complex, the budgetary process can be more elaborate and take more time to move from budget requests, to authorisation and then construction. The capital budget itself has two distinct elements. First, the total costs of the projects over the periods of construction and, second, the consequent costs of operating them in the years after their completion. Also, a wider range of officers is involved (including planners, architects, engineers), often involving contractors (written specifications of projects, contracts, tendering, controlling execution of contracts). Exhibit 5.3 illustrates a capital budget, distinguishing between capital cash payments and operating cash payments.

Exhibit 5.3 Capital budget of the City of Eutopia, for fiscal years 20x2–20x6

£000			Schedule of Planned Capital Cash Payments						Operating costs of capital projects	
Total project cost	Project name	Details of project	20x2	20x3	20x4	20x5	20x6	Expected year of completion	20x3	20x4
3,050	Project A		1,560	630	350	–	–	20x3	–	180
2,100	Project B		580	1,340	–	–	–	20x3	–	140
1,500	Project C		1,500	–	–	–	–	20x4	90	157
4,500	Project D		–	–	3,750	750	–	20x5	–	–
6,300	Project E		–	–	3,500	2,000	800	20x6	–	–
			3,640	1,970	7,600	2,750	800		90	477

City of Eutopia Capital Budget
Years ended [*date*], 20x2–20x6

The rational approach to all decisions about service provision in governments is to appraise them before they are included in strategic planning and budget requests. The size and complexity of capital projects, especially in their wide-ranging impacts, and the fact that they naturally have more of a separable focus than the operating activities, mean that specialist appraisal is often necessary. The economic risks associated with them are often high and their visibility means that the political risks are often also high. Capital projects continually go wrong (construction and operating cost overruns are common, as are delays) despite sophisticated analysis, but that serves to emphasise the analysis needs to be improved. There is an additional factor that necessitates specialist appraisal techniques, though: time. The capital costs of a project can be incurred over more than one year and the tangible benefits can extend well into the future. The time dimension adds particular forms of complexity to the analysis, in addition to the increasing risks and uncertainties as the time horizon lengthens. There is what to the uninitiated accountant might seem a paradox: although total cost overruns are common, in the early years projects are commonly underspent. This is explained by the overoptimism of engineers and other technical specialists in judging how much time projects take from initiation to completion.

Capital project appraisal requires estimates of the amounts, timing, quantifiable risks and unquantifiable uncertainties of the inputs, outputs and outcomes of each project. In a for-profit or not-for-profit organisation, the inputs, outputs and outcomes are its private ones (some of which may in essence be public ones forced on to the private body by government regulations), but, in governments, all identifiable consequences of the project are relevant – private and public. In private organisations, the inputs, outputs and outcomes can typically be, and in definitive textbook discussion will be, quantified in financial amounts, though the financial consequences of outcomes are still difficult to assess and defend (for example, when human life is being valued). In governments, the necessarily wider, public consequences of a project (often termed the social benefits and costs) tend to mean that there is less financial quantification, less quantification in non-financial terms and more reliance on qualitative assessment and greater emphasis on politics, if not in the appraisal then in the generation and authorisation of a project. There is, however, a long-standing, if still controversial, economic technique that attempts to increase the amount of financial quantification to the largest possible and, along with non-financial quantification, to reduce the amount of qualitative assessment to the smallest possible: cost–benefit analysis.

Having estimated the amounts, timing, quantifiable risks and unquantifiable uncertainties of the inputs, outputs and outcomes, the cash flows occurring in the future are discounted (using a discount factor) to a common point (usually the time of the appraisal), which is known as the calculation of present values. The present values of all amounts are then compared by calculating the net present value of the benefits (net of the costs) to judge whether the outputs exceed the inputs by an appropriate amount in the light of the estimated outcomes. There are variations on these calculations for special cases (such as the use of equivalent annual values when projects of different lives are being compared, or terminal values).

In estimating future cash flows, the market prices of inputs and outputs can be used, but not, of course, from bad markets, as they do not then measure opportunity costs well. Some government projects will be because markets are bad (unemployment in labour markets, underemployment of finance and capital goods, quasi-monopolists in all markets, effects of taxation). Surrogates for good market prices are known as shadow prices and can be estimated in a number of ways:

- surveys that ask what people would be willing to pay for a specific improvement in a service – 'How much extra would you pay to travel this specific journey by taxi compared to the bus?', for example

- observations of what people do pay when faced with a clear choice between two forms of a service with different costs and benefits – how much people pay to travel the specific journey by taxi rather than bus.

The choice of discount factor is a difficult one and the theory on what the appropriate rate is is contradictory. The factor trades off future net benefits and current net benefits. It can be broken into two elements: a person's preference for the future against the present (referred to as time preference) and the risks and uncertainty of the future against the present. The latter includes the unknown effects of future general price changes on the value of money. This problem is dealt with in practice by expressing all cash flows in money valued at the date of the appraisal (colloquially, 'today's prices'). This is known as expressing cash flows in real terms. As long as the discount factor is also in real terms, the appraisal is sound.

Time preference and other uncertainties are more difficult to deal with. Individuals', markets' and populations' rates of time preference can be very different. When the present is preferred to the future, high discount factors are observable, but when the future is to be emphasised, then they are low. Good markets take the different rates of time preferences of the marketmakers and turn them into a market rate. As with market prices for inputs and outputs, it is not necessarily appropriate for a government project. For example, a government project may be just because the markets are (using high discount factors) taking a short-term view that the government believes will have serious long-term consequences (and so prefers low discount factors).

In good money markets, observable rates (combinations of time preference and risk and uncertainty) are available. Which ones should be used, however, remains difficult. Rates for private sector investment are expected to be higher than for government investment, if only to reflect the usual expectation of higher risk. In a government project, an argument for using the higher rate is that this allows an unbiased comparison to be made between the private and public sectors. By holding the discount rate equal all other aspects of the project can be compared to appraise which sector is better at providing the service. A counter-argument is that, if a government can raise finance more cheaply than the private sector, that is a good reason for a project to be undertaken in the public sector, so the lower rate should be used to reflect the inherent bias in the two forms of investment. One response to this counter-argument is that the risks of public investment will rise as its proportion of national income rises, which may happen because the increased public investment crowds out private investment.

The amounts, timing, quantifiable risks and discount factors all have ranges of possibilities, the best estimates of which can seriously influence the acceptability or otherwise of a project. The practical response is to include a sensitivity analysis, which identifies a few of the more important probabilities. Calculating the effects of different but plausible discount factors on net present values is an obvious practice. Exhibit 5.4 is an appraisal of Project A based only on cash flows, using two discount rates to provide the sensitivity analysis.

Exhibit 5.4 Appraisal of Capital Project A for the City of Eutopia: traditional method and only cash flows

City of Eutopia Capital Project A
At [*beginning date*], 20x2

The cash flows for this project relate to completing the project (capital cash outflows until 20x4) and the cash outflows less cash inflows to operate the project for 26 years starting in 20x4. The estimated timing and amounts are shown below (all cash flows assumed to take place at the end of each year). At the end of the 26 years, the project will be sold for a negligible amount.

In [beginning date] 20x2 £000	Net present value of future cash flows		Cash flows at year ending [date]			
	6% discount factor	8% discount factor	20x2	20x3	20x4	25 years from 20x5 onwards
Capital cash flows	–	–	(1,560)	(630)	(350)	–
Operating cash flows	–	–	–	–	(180)	(180) a year
Total cash flows	(4,306)	(3,817)	(1,560)	(630)	(530)	(180) a year

The net present values are negative (£4,306,000 at 6 per cent and £3,817,000 at 8 per cent), as would be expected from a project financed ultimately by taxation. The appraisal can then be extended to include social costs and benefits, which are often difficult but not impossible to assign monetary values to. The project will obviously provide benefits – otherwise it would not have been put in the capital budget – but it may also incur social costs, perhaps in damage to the environment or inconvenience to those living close to it. Monetary values for these net social benefits have been incorporated in Exhibit 5.5, which significantly change the net present values of the project (positive £86,000 at 6 per cent and negative £361,000 at 8 per cent).

Exhibit 5.5 Appraisal of Capital Project A for the City of Eutopia: traditional method, cash flows and net social benefits

City of Eutopia Capital Project A
At [*beginning date*], 20x2

The cash flows for this project relate to completing the project (capital cash outflows until 20x4) and the cash outflows less cash inflows to operate the project for 26 years starting in 20x4. The estimated timing and amounts are shown below (all cash flows assumed to take place at the end of each year). At the end of the 26 years, the project will be sold for a negligible amount. The net social benefits are evaluated at £400,000 a year for 26 years, beginning in 20x4.

In [beginning date] 20x2 £000	Present value of future cash flows		Cash flows at year ending [date]			
	6% discount factor	8% discount factor	20x2	20x3	20x4	25 years from 20x5 onwards
Capital cash flows	–	–	(1,560)	(630)	(350)	–
Operating cash flows	–	–	–	–	(180)	(180) a year
Net social benefits	–	–	–	–	400	400 a year
Total	86	(361)	(1,560)	(630)	(130)	220 a year

A radical approach to capital projects was developed by the UK government in the 1990s, known as the private finance initiative (PFI). On the face of it, its name does not reflect its essence well as borrowing from the private sector had always been a common way to directly finance capital projects (earmarked borrowing) and indirectly finance them (increase general levels of debt). What is new here is that the private sector is used to not just finance a capital project directly but also build and operate it, in return for a fixed payment every year for, say, 30 years (known as the primary concession period). The name of this policy is now clearly appropriate: by involving the private sector in many more aspects of a capital project, it is asserting that, during the primary concession period, the projects are privately owned and operated. This is an assertion that financial accounting and reporting can contest, but it was an important part of how the policy developed. At the end of the primary concession period, the payments stop and the ownership and management of the project is taken over by the government.

The economic essence of these capital projects, when compared with a traditional project, is the shift in risk to the private sector; the concomitant returns are reflected in the annual payments. As there are important parts of the projects that continue to be owned by the government, some of the explicit risks are retained by the public sector (as well as the implicit risks and rewards of all projects that are 'too big to fail'). The premise of these projects is that the services provided are better than under a traditional project because there is a better sharing of risk between the public and private sectors. This premise is given added emphasis because there is an increase in the visibility of the risk in many capital projects. Also, it deals with another fundamental problem arising from the traditional method: the great enthusiasm with which capital projects are embarked on often contrasts markedly with the lower enthusiasm there is for their subsequent routine maintenance. The nature of PFI projects forces the quantifiable risks and the expected costs of adequate routine maintenance throughout a project's life to be made explicit right at the beginning when the project decision is made.

The PFI in the UK only set the broad parameters of the individual contracts for the projects, not the details of each one, which were left to each governmental organisation to negotiate with its contractors. In practice, there were many variations in the sharing of risk, including novel ways of using notional revenues (for example, by tracking the traffic on toll-free roads and generating shadow tolls to determine the payments to contractors).

A PFI project requires explicit comparison with the traditional method. A significant difference in the costs of the two methods will be the extra costs of contracting and monitoring the PFI method. Under both methods, the necessarily detailed specifications of contracts impose costs on the government and on the contractors, including on the unsuccessful bidders. Under the traditional method, however, these only relate to the capital aspects of the project; under the PFI method, they extend to financing and operating aspects, for the whole of the primary concession period, including the terms of the transfer of the project to the government at the end of it. A problem is that these additional costs are explicit while the organisational costs of operating capital projects under the traditional method are more likely to be unquantifiable.

The problems under the traditional method in choosing between private sector and public sector rates for the appropriate discount factor are highlighted when comparing it with the PFI. Using a private rate in the PFI method, while using a lower government rate in the traditional one, might in itself determine which is the better method. The unquantifiable uncertainties of both methods are then added to the appraisal, qualitatively.

Exhibit 5.6 shows the appraisal of Project A as a PFI project using only cash flows. At a 6 per cent discount rate, the traditional method produces a better net present value, while at 8 per cent, the PFI alternative is better. This kind of sensitivity to the discount factor when choosing between the two methods is not unusual.

Exhibit 5.6 Appraisal of Capital Project A for the City of Eutopia: private finance initiative method and cash flows only

City of Eutopia Capital Project A
At [*beginning date*], 20x2
The project operates from 20x4 and the cash payments to the contractor are £250,000 in 20x4 and £420,000 a year for the 25 years thereafter. The estimated timing and amounts are shown below (all cash flows assumed to take place at the end of each year). At the end of the 26 years, Eutopia will take over the project from the contractor, but will sell it for a negligible amount.

In [beginning date] 20x2 £000	Present value of future cash flows		Cash flows at year ending [date]			
	6% discount factor	8% discount factor	20x2	20x3	20x4	25 years from 20x5 onwards
Capital cash flows	–	–	–	–	–	–
PFI cash payments	–	–	–	–	(250)	(420) a year
Total	(4,463)	(3,493)	–	–	(250)	(420) a year

If we now add the net social benefits to the PFI project, the traditional method is still to be preferred at a 6 per cent discount rate. PFI projects, however, are also intended to shift some of the risk to the contractors. Exhibit 5.7 introduces the net social benefits and the risk transfer evaluated at £25,000 a year for each of the years of operation. This changes the decision – at a 6 per cent discount rate, the PFI project is the preferred option.

Separating the capital budget from the operating budget and then linking them is rational and commonplace in governments, not-for-profits and for-profits. There are notable cases (the US Federal government is one), however, in which the separation is not made and this practice is vigorously supported. The arguments can only be understood when the accounting basis of the budget is included. In the US Federal government, there is obligation-based budgeting, contrasted with accrual-based budgeting. The central argument of obligation-based budgeting is that the cost of capital projects is scored in full in the budget at the time the decision is made to authorise the budgets for those projects. This is seen as important in controlling the politicians who authorise the budgets. In contrast, accrual-based budgeting scores the capital costs over the life of the assets, through the depreciation charge, in the operating budget.

Exhibit 5.7 **Appraisal of Capital Project A for the City of Eutopia: private finance initiative method, cash flows and net social benefits/risk transfer**

City of Eutopia Capital Project A
At [*beginning date*], 20x2

The project operates from 20x4 and the cash payments to the contractor are £250,000 in 20x4 and £420,000 a year for the 25 years thereafter. The estimated timing and amounts are shown below (all cash flows assumed to take place at the end of each year). At the end of the 26 years, Eutopia will take over the project from the contractor, but will sell it for a negligible amount. The net social benefits and risk transfer are evaluated at £425,000 a year for 26 years, beginning in 20x4.

In [beginning date] 20x2 £000	Present value of future cash flows		Cash flows at year ending [date]			
	6% discount factor	8% discount factor	20x2	20x3	20x4	25 years from 20x5 onwards
Capital cash flows	–	–	–	–	–	–
PFI cash payments	–	–	–	–	(250)	(420) a year
Net social benefits/ risk transfer	–	–	–	–	425	425 a year
Total	198	–	–	–	175	5 a year

The counter-argument to accrual-based budgeting is that it also scores the full amount in the capital budget at the time of the decision, in practice, this can have less force because of the different ways that a separate operating budget and a separate capital budget might be financed. If the government decided that the capital budget could be financed by borrowing, while the operating budget had to be financed by taxation, then, from the politicians' point of view, scoring against the capital budget hurts much less than scoring against the operating budget. Thus, the obligation-based budget is a single (unitary) budget that scores all costs – operating and capital – at the time they are obligated.

Accrual-based budgeting might respond to this argument by insisting that the capital budget can be controlled to the same degree as the operating budget, but perhaps in different ways. Part of this could be not conceding that the capital budget can be financed by borrowing.

5.3 Line item incremental budgets

Line items are the accountant's classification of revenues, expenses, assets, liabilities and cash flows within the operating statement, balance sheet and cash flow statement. In operating budgets, they are primarily classifications of what is to be bought with the money being requested (inputs, of course, though the budgets will also include line items of revenues). Line item budgeting can be used whatever structure is used but they most are most naturally associated with organisational structures.

There are very different ways, however, of combining organisational structures and line items. The structures can range from highly aggregated to detailed, as can the line items. Exhibit 5.8 gives an example of highly aggregated line items.

Exhibit 5.8 **Annual budget for the City of Eutopia, for fiscal year 20x2, based on gross expenditure by organisational structure: basis for pie charts of how much of the budget each department spends**

£000	City of Eutopia Budget Year ended [date], 20x2			
	Actual 20x0	Original budget 20x1	Revised budget 20x1	Budget 20x2
Gross expenditure				
Corporate Services	7,050	6,500	6,750	7,500
Education Department	22,820	24,500	26,250	28,000
Police Department	20,560	24,000	23,500	27,500
Social Services Department	13,920	14,500	14,500	16,250
Transport Department	6,920	8,000	8,500	9,400
Total gross expenditure	71,270	77,500	79,500	88,650
Charges for services				
Corporate Services	–	–	–	–
Education Department	2,320	2,500	2,750	3,000
Police Department	5,450	6,000	6,300	7,500
Social Services Department	1,670	1,500	1,600	1,750
Transport Department	1,890	2,000	2,100	2,500
Total gross revenues	11,330	12,000	12,750	14,750
Total net expenditure	59,940	65,500	66,750	73,900

Exhibit 5.9 gives the same budget, but summarised according to what the budget will buy and how it will be financed. This provides a useful overview of, for example, the extent to which employee costs dominate the budget.

Exhibit 5.9 **Annual budget for the City of Eutopia, for fiscal year 20x2, based on gross expenditure and gross revenues by line items: basis for pie charts of what the government as a whole buys with its budget and how it pays for it**

£000	City of Eutopia Budget Year ended [date], 20x2			
	Actual 20x0	Original budget 20x1	Revised budget 20x1	Budget 20x2
Gross expenditure				
Employees	58,590	63,250	64,000	68,700
Premises	5,980	6,640	7,240	10,380
Transport	4,320	4,500	4,900	5,600
Supplies	1,230	1,450	1,380	1,570
Interest	1,150	1,360	1,980	2,400
Total gross expenditure	71,270	77,500	79,500	88,650
Gross revenues				
Taxes	30,460	35,000	28,880	37,900
Grants	24,570	28,000	29,000	33,000
Donations	2,350	2,500	2,100	3,000
Charges for services	11,330	12,000	12,750	14,750
Total gross revenues	68,710	77,500	72,730	88,650
Total government net expenditure	2,560	–	6,770	–

A highly aggregated devolved budget could be such that each department, of many, has a single line item budget. Alternatively, as shown in Exhibit 5.10, a detailed specification of a highly centralised budget can be used.

Exhibit 5.10 **Detailed line items in the annual budget for the Social Services Department of the City of Eutopia, for fiscal year 20x2**

| Social Services Department Budget, City of Eutopia | | | | |
| Year ended [*date*], 20x2 | | | | |
£000	*Actual 20x0*	*Original budget 20x1*	*Revised budget 20x1*	*Budget 20x2*
Gross expenditure				
Employees				
Salaries	8,465	9,255	9,370	11,040
Payroll taxes	340	390	520	630
Pension contributions	985	1,020	1,175	1,280
Wages	1,560	1,700	1,700	1,750
Payroll taxes	20	25	25	30
Pension contributions	90	110	110	120
Total employees	11,460	12,500	12,900	14,850

In incremental budgets, the request for the coming year is justified in terms of it involving only marginal changes compared with the previous year's budget. When political scientist Aaron Wildavsky observed this practice in the early 1960s, at the beginning of his celebrated work on the politics of budgetary processes, he called it 'incrementalism'. There was nothing new about the practice, but his nomenclature has stuck, even though the word misleadingly implies that the practice must always lead to budgets increasing year on year. The essence of this feature of budgeting is not that budgets *must* always increase but that budgets are justified on the basis that they involve only marginal changes compared with those from previous years – the changes may, in principle, even be decrements.

Exhibit 5.11 is an example of how an incremental budget is produced, emphasising typical justifications for the marginal changes. The awareness that it is the incremental changes that are controllable leads to budget statement formats that attempt to isolate the various reasons for the changes. To the original budget for the current year (Column 2) are added the effects of increased costs and pay awards (Columns 4 and 5) and the amounts for committed growth (Columns 6–8) to produce the committed budget figure (Column 9). In this case, if the base level of activity implied by the expenses included in Column 2 is to be undertaken the following year, then this will require the amounts shown in Column 9. The only incremental items are the amounts for further growth in Columns 10 and 11. If the existing base is not reviewed, then they are the only amounts that can be controlled.

An accountant would criticise incremental budgets by pointing out that last year's budget, when it was authorised, was a prediction and a past prediction is

Exhibit 5.11 Analysis of increments in the annual budget for the Social Services Department of the City of Eutopia, for fiscal year 20x2: committed growth

£000	Original budget 20x1	Revised budget 20x1	Pay awards	Other increased costs	Full year of employees appointed in 20x1	Operating costs of capital projects	Other	Committed budget 20x2	Operating costs of capital projects	Committed budget 20x3
					Department A Budget: Committed Growth Years ended [date], 20x2 and 20x3					
[1]	[2]	[3]	[4]	[5]	[6]	[7]	[8]	[9]	[10]	[11]
Employees:										
Salaries	9,255	9,370	315	–	780	–	–	10,350	–	12,350
Payroll taxes	390	520	15	–	30	–	–	435	–	650
Pension contributions	1,020	1,175	55	–	1,090	–	–	2,165	–	3,400
Total salaries	10,665	11,065	385	–	1,900	–	–	12,950	–	16,400

not the best base to use to make a current prediction – it is better to compare last year's budget with the actual net spending, to test how good that prediction was (which would provide a guide as to how good the government is at making predictions) and use verified information about last year to make the prediction for this year. The purpose of Column 3 is to produce a more up-to-date prediction of what last year's spending will be. In producing this, however, there is a difficult practical problem that profoundly affects the nature of the budget cycle. The problem is that the budget is being produced in advance of the fiscal year, its final stages being in months 10, 11 and 12 of the previous fiscal year. The revised budget for that previous fiscal year – the base – is therefore limited to predictions for that year being made at the end of months 7, 8 or 9, depending on how efficient the accounting system is in producing interim figures for spending. In addition, such predictions have to take account of the results of the surge of activity that takes place at the end of fiscal years in producing final figures for the year. These practical problems mean that, while the revised budget for the previous year does provide useful information, it is rarely a substitute for figures of actual spending.

Exhibit 5.12 gives a summary of the budget, showing not only committed growth but also any uncommitted growth, including marginal changes that are cuts made in last year's budget, so uncommitted growth is instead a reduction in spending.

With growth, the managers more naturally take the last year's budget as given and then identify how increased spending on current ways of providing services can improve them, in addition to increased spending on different ways of providing improved services. With cuts, it is much more likely that the decreased

Exhibit 5.12 Increment in the annual budget for the City of Eutopia, for fiscal year 20x2: committed and uncommitted growth

£000	Original budget 20x1	Committed growth	Uncommitted growth	Budget 20x2
	City of Eutopia Budget Year ended [date], 20x2			
Gross expenditure				
Employees	63,250	4,150	1,300	68,700
Premises	6,640	2,490	1,250	10,380
Transport	4,500	850	250	5,600
Supplies	1,450	270	(150)	1,570
Interest	1,360	540	200	2,400
Total gross expenditure	77,500	8,300	2,850	88,650
Gross revenues				
Taxes	35,000	–	2,900	37,900
Grants	28,000	–	5,000	33,000
Donations	2,500	–	500	3,000
Charges for services	12,000	–	2,750	14,750
Total gross revenues	77,500	–	11,150	88,650
Total government net expenditure	–	8,300	8,300	–

spending (on current ways of providing services or on different ways of doing so) will have deep impacts on the base itself. Put another way, when there are to be cuts in budgets, how far must the base be re-examined?

A recurring way to answer that question is for the central controllers to ask budgetholders for a schedule of ways in which they would make, say, a 5 per cent, 10 per cent and 20 per cent cut. Such a method is not as linear as it may seem. A 10 per cent cut is not necessarily made up of what would have been cut under the 5 per cent limit plus the balance – the size of the cut can shift the priorities. The larger the cut, the more likely it is to affect the remaining base. Moreover, while the method may be to ask for ways to respond to across-the-board cuts, it does not necessarily lead to the same cuts being made in all departments or programmes. Across-the-board cuts, when expressed in such a way, ignores the differing outputs and outcomes in different departments as it can be assumed that the relationships between inputs, outputs and outcomes would not be uniform. The imperative for such kinds of cuts broadly comes when there are financial crises that dominate all other considerations, including political sensitivities.

A budgetary cycle that began by asking budgetholders what they would do if their budgets were reduced by 20 per cent compared with the previous year could be called an incremental system of 80 per cent base budgeting. A logical extension of such a method would be to ask budgetholders what they would do if their individual budgets were reduced to zero, hence a zero-base budgeting system.

5.4 Output measurement and outcomes

The budgets in the previous exhibits focus on inputs. Explicit consideration, including measurement, of outputs and outcomes is demanded by politicians, taxpayers and service users; the task for the accountant is to link them with budgets. For all the reasons that performance measurement is very challenging, this task is also very challenging.

The traditional measures of cost per head (student, client, patient) and cost per thousand population link input and output and are useful, but they are very crude proxies for outcomes and are not the kinds of performance measures used by politicians, taxpayers or service users. The kinds of direct output measures that are so used have to be simple and very specific and they are, therefore, unsuited to representing the complexities of planning, execution and monitoring of service provision. The typical resolution of this dilemma is for budgets to be accompanied by a few output measures of incremental changes in performance, only therefore *implying* causality between inputs, outputs and outcomes rather than *asserting* it.

Exhibit 5.13 shows how some measures might be appended to the budget.

Exhibit 5.13 **Output measures added to the annual budget for Secondary Schools, Education Department, City of Eutopia, year ended (*date*) 20x2**

Education Department, City of Eutopia Budget Year ended [*date*], 20x2	Actual 20x0	Original budget 20x1	Budget 20x2
Cost per student	£4,650	£4,800	£5,100
Cost per thousand population	£850	£890	£950
14-year-olds:			
English:			
A	71%	69%	70%
B	18%	19%	20%
C	11%	12%	10%
Mathematics:			
A	58%	60%	65%
B	20%	22%	25%
C	22%	18%	10%
Science:			
A	77%	78%	80%
B	17%	17%	15%
C	6%	5%	5%
16-year-olds:			
5 or more A or B grades	44%	44%	45%

5.5 Zero-base reviews

Incremental budgeting is a description of how budgets typically are, and long have been, compiled. It invites the criticism that rational budgets should not take last year – the base – as the starting point. The accountant's criticism that the cycle of incremental budgets, from original budget to original budget, is unbroken by verified details of actual spending is part of this. The wider criticism of using last year as the base is that it assumes the base was the best allocation of resources, with only marginal changes needing to be made to it.

A logical extension of this criticism is that the budget should have no basis in last year's spending and everything in it should be wholly justified as part of the overall allocation of resources – that the budget should have a zero base. As a warning for budgets to not simply assume that last year's budget is a sound base, this idea is very old. As the essence of a comprehensive system of budgeting, known as zero-base budgeting, it dates from the 1960s in the USA. In its clearest form, it was packaged in the private sector and then, in the 1970s particularly, was experimented with in some US governments. It has been spasmodically resurrected in some forms in different settings, including in the UK, but, as a comprehensive system, it did not come to dominate budgetary practices.

One reason is that, despite its unassailable logic, the logic of a zero base relates to the artifice we know as the annual budget, not the reality of government activity. This budget is crucial to control in all its forms and, of course, does reflect a natural cycle (though, when that cycle is assumed to begin is artificial), but it is still artificial. Government revenues and spending (and all other government activities that do not have direct financial effects) flow in real time, not discrete periods, much less at annual rests. The logic of zero-base budgeting is not logical in the context of most governments most of the time. To impose an annual artifice on the flow of government is necessary, but it is usually not logical to impose it annually with a zero base. The costs of generating the necessary information each year, about all government activities, are also high.

It is necessary continually to re-examine departments or programmes from the point of view of outcomes, outputs and inputs. In incremental budgeting – with added emphasis because it can proceed for years, from one prediction to the next, without being grounded in what is actually happening – redundant budgets can build up and then be used for less than optimal spending. Of course, the service departments will anyway continually re-examine their services, which may well include financial effects. Also, the practice of performance auditing will continually contribute to the same re-examinations.

There may be a recurring setting in which a zero-base budget is called for. A new administration – particularly one taking over after a long period in opposition – would not naturally base its first budget on the previous year's as that would have been the budget of the previous administration. The commonsense appeal of zero-base budgeting might be used, though the enthusiasm for using the technique beyond the first year will naturally pall.

FURTHER READING

Burrows, G. and Syme, B. (2000) 'Zero-base budgeting: origins and pioneers', *Abacus*, 36(2), 226–41.

Edwards, P. and Shaoul, J. (2003) 'Controlling the PFI process in schools: a case study of the Pimlico Project', *Policy and Politics*, 31(3): 371–85.

Froud, J. (2003) 'The Private Finance Initiative: risk, uncertainty and the State', *Accounting, Organizations and Society*, 28(6): 567–89.

Ismail, S. and Pendlebury, M. (2006) 'The Private Finance Initiative (PFI) in schools: the experience of users', *Financial Accountability and Management*, 22(4): 381–404.

Jones, L. and McCaffery, J. (2005), 'Reform of the planning, programming, budgeting system, and management control in the U.S. Department of Defense: insights from budget theory', *Public Budgeting and Finance*, Fall: 1–19.

Makowsky, M. and Wagner, R. (2009) 'From scholarly idea to budgetary institution: the emergence of cost–benefit analysis', *Constitutional Political Economy*, 20: 57–70.

Martin, S., Rice, N. and Smith, P. (2008) 'Does health care spending improve health outcomes? Evidence from English programme budgeting data', *Journal of Health Economics*, 27: 826–42.

Chapter 6

Budgetary control

Government budgets are important to external accountability, but are also used as an important part of internal control. Indeed, management accounting systems, and wider management control systems, are structured around budgeting. Budgetary control is a dominant function of accounting, but it can be exercised in different ways.

6.1 Central financial control

The traditional and enduring view of budgetary control is that, as money is at the heart of it, those responsible for the finances of the organisation as a whole focus on direct and detailed control of the spending of the individual budgetholders in the spending departments. This focus on detailed control of inputs is not to the exclusion of control of outputs and outcomes, but it significantly underemphasises them in the budgetary process. The line item, incremental budget – based on the organisational structure – is the natural form for the budget to take in this method of control. It is in the interests of those responsible for the organisation as a whole to exercise control in this way, but it is often also in the interests of the politicians and the public, whose money is being spent. Whenever, for certain groups of people, the imperative is control of money, the direct and detailed control of spending by departments by the centre of the organisation is the appropriate method.

Control of money can always be assumed to be an imperative, but there are times and other circumstances in which there are more choices available that affect outputs and outcomes and so warrant a subtler balance between the control of inputs and outputs. One theme has been to have more devolved systems of budgetary control in which, overall, the broad control of inputs and outputs is maintained by the centre, but detailed controls are devolved. The various elements of budgetary control can be combined in many different ways, however, and it is not possible to be categorical about when one comprehensive method is more appropriate than another, but it is possible to define the elements of central financial control and then identify typical ways in which these elements can be changed.

Direct and detailed central financial control is an ideal form of control from an accountant's point of view and was taken in this way in the early development of modern governments, using the UK government as a model. It was associated (notwithstanding the fact that the size of modern governments' budgets grew at unprecedented rates) with the idea that public money had to be spent on the cheapest that money could buy, especially for routine, recurrent spending. The main elements of this central financial control have been called the classic rules of budgetary theory:

- unity
- balanced budget
- non-hypothecation of revenues and gross budget principle
- annuality
- specification.

All of them are familiar, to some degree or other, in governments around the world. Calling them 'rules' fits best in situations that are typical in continental Europe, for example, in which they are embodied in the law, from constitutional law down to regulations. In the UK, in contrast, they are principles that are, for the most part, practised rather than stated in generalised form, even though the practices are pervasive. Thus, the principles are, in this sense, typical of management accounting rather than financial accounting, being mainly unregulated. One consequence of this in Anglophone accounting is that, as pervasive and familiar as the principles are, there is a wide variety of practices. There have been periods when trends away from a strict application of the principles are detectable, at least in ways of thinking, but it is important to understand that the traditional incentives for central financial control remain strong.

The principle of unity is that there is only one budget for the organisation as a whole and spending can only take place against that budget, which is putting all the eggs in one basket and controlling the basket. The effect of that is there is no off-budget financing of any kind. There are no budgetholders who can, in the way that a business can, use their own revenues to finance future spending, whether operating or investment spending. The activities of the budgetholders are budget-financed not self-financed. Unity offers the possibility that the centre of the organisation – represented by the politicians and central financial controllers – can make the necessary trade-offs between all budgetholders across the departments and programmes to determine who spends, how much and on what.

This overall budget has to be paid for and it is up to the central financial controllers to ensure that the finance is forthcoming. A key decision is about the mix of borrowing and taxation. The second classic rule is to balance the budget, meaning to finance the budget wholly by taxation. This is a strict control, in commonsense terms, whether the common sense relates to each of us as individuals or to organisations in that the coming year's services are to be paid for by the coming year's taxes. Whether the government can afford to spend what its budget authorises it to spend or not is a matter of whether it can collect the necessary taxes or not. For a narrow, but enduring, sense of control, the sooner it can collect those taxes the better.

Governments financed by taxation sever the connection between spending on services free at the point of delivery and paying for them. The strict balanced budget is the central financial controller's way of re-establishing the link. The taxpayers will ultimately pay and the balanced budget forces them to pay when the spending takes place. Taxpayers may not have the incentives to be concerned about future generations of taxpayers, even of future years' taxpayers, and politicians are endowed with finite, and short, time horizons. The central financial controller uses the balanced budget to add fiscal responsibility to the budgetary process. The orthodoxy of unbalanced budgets in situations in which the imperative is to balance the economy necessarily weakens central financial control.

Unity of the budget (so that spending can only take place against that budget) is reinforced by two other principles: non-hypothecation of revenues and gross budget principle. The first of these means that revenues, including tax revenues, are collected to finance the organisation's budget as a whole. Consequently, the organisation's spending is determined by the budget, not the source of finance. A particular tax, for example, is not hypothecated in *advance* of its collection for a particular purpose. The reason this is important for central control is that, at the point when a tax is hypothecated – perhaps by passing a specific law – the control of how that tax will be spent is handed over to the service to which it is assigned. Any subsequent increase or decrease in the revenues from that tax, perhaps because of circumstances outside of the control of the government or budgetholder, will automatically be applied to that service regardless of need in relation to the services of the government as a whole.

The non-hypothecation of taxes separates the right of taxpayers to receive particular governmental services from their duty to pay taxes. An illustrative example is in a recurring, if usually futile, challenge to the authority of government by a taxpayer who is content with everything that the government does except for one service. For example, the taxpayer might be a pacifist who disapproves of contributing to defence. The taxpayer, using the budget, then attempts to calculate the amount of the tax bill that is being appropriated for defence, deducts that amount from the bill and pays the balance. The logic may be sound to the taxpayer, but the legitimate response of the government will be to imprison the taxpayer. The duty to pay the tax bill is wholly separate from the appropriation of the subsequent tax revenues.

The gross budget principle means that the authorised budget for each budget-holder separates budgeted spending from any budgeted revenues (which, by excluding central forms of finance such as taxation and borrowing will be fewer, leaving a budget of net spending). The point of this gross budget is that the centre is determining, separately, how the budget will be spent and how the budgetholder's revenues will be collected. The consequence is that, if the budgetholder collects revenues in addition to those budgeted, the revenues cannot be spent by the budgetholder. The additional revenues cannot be netted off against additional spending to produce a neutral effect on the budgetholder's budget as a whole – the two amounts must instead be kept gross. In effect, the additional revenues are for the centre to use to finance the overall budget of the organisation, not for the individual budgetholder, even though that budget-holder might have been responsible for identifying and collecting those revenues.

The principle of annuality is that the authorised spending must take place during the fiscal year. There is an annual reckoning of spending against the budget, which has explicit, intended consequences. If there is overspending, there is a range of possible penalties, perhaps including personal liability of the budget-holder for the overspent amount. If there is underspending, the unspent amount is lost by the budgetholder and surrendered to the centre (hence the term 'lapsing budgets' is sometimes used). In principle, therefore, annuality requires government departments to spend the budget – neither more nor less. In practice, though, the political and managerial consequences of overspending are more strongly felt than the consequences of underspending, however strongly they may be felt by service recipients. This is true of the central financial controllers, but it is natural in any setting where resources are scarce.

The particular significance of the annual financial reckoning is not its length but that the reckoning is not continuous – that is, the budgetholder is not simultaneously taking account of every financial effect on the organisation at the time each amount is spent. If there were a continuous budgeting and accounting system, there would be no budget in the conventional sense and there would be no annuality.

Major parts of budgets will not be affected by annuality. Much of the budget for employees will be determined by the employment contracts, not month-to-month budgetary control. Although such line items can amount to large percentages of budgets, the line items that are affected by annuality can amount to large sums of money.

There are a number of advantages of annuality for central financial control, which help to ensure that public money is spent in the public interest as determined by the government as a whole, not by individual budgetholders. Some budgetholders may underspend, while others may overspend. Moreover, it is common for there to be substantial amounts within budgets that are not strictly controllable by the budgetholders. To take the two extremes, underspending could have been fortuitous and overspending inevitable, for many reasons. It is the responsibility of the central controllers to finance the overspendings, so it is natural to want to have the underspendings available for that purpose. Anyone who is responsible for the financial control of budgetholders (rather than the outputs and outcomes of their spending) has, therefore, a natural incentive to impose annuality. Such a person actually does not have to be a financial controller.

Another advantage of annuality for central control is that a budgetholder could not use underspendings (either fortuitous or planned ones) to create reserves over many years, which might then be used to subvert central policies. For example, such reserves might be used to increase the gap between the wealthiest and the poorest schools, which might not be a policy of the government as a whole.

The principle of specification is that the centre specifies in great detail what budgetholders can buy with their budgets. The same idea can be applied to outputs and outcomes, but the principle is then developed in the context of the specification of line items. This form of control is the reason that government budgets can be such forbiddingly detailed documents. In its extreme form, the budget specifies the line items in detail and prohibits changing the line items during the year, but also prohibits transferring budgets from one line item to another (known as virement, the French word for transferring). In practice, however, the principle requires a useful balance to be struck between maintaining the central control of inputs but at a level of detail that is manageable, given that most centres of governments cannot usefully control every transaction.

In striking the balance, specification is often accompanied by some virement but within written rules agreed with the centre. These rules might distinguish between the virement that can be at the discretion of the budgetholder and the virement that needs central approval. So, for example, virement under the discretion of the budgetholder might be restricted to transfers that do not involve changes of central political policy, novel or contentious forms of spending, large additional amounts of spending, liabilities or commitments to spend in future years that otherwise would not occur, such as transfers from capital budgets to hire employees or transfers from a supplies budget to a capital project with future operating spending implications, or transfers from projects financed by external sources, such as grants or in partnership arrangements.

6.2 Devolved forms of financial control

Direct and detailed control of the spending of the individual budgetholders in the spending departments by the centre of an organisation has potential weaknesses. In large, multipurpose governments, such control challenges the ability of the centre to know in detail how to execute its strategies because it includes knowing service recipients' demands and how to satisfy them. It is better to leave the budgetholders and their specialists to implement policies and deal with the uncertainties of specific and general price changes and the technologies of each service. This is most obviously a problem in national or supranational governments. The effects of geographical distance and diversity may be mitigated by the easy gathering and storage of electronic data, but not completely. The extreme form of central financial control is to have a centrally planned economy, the premises of which have been discredited.

In less ambitious contexts of central control, it can deflect attention away from outputs and outcomes and discourage managers from managing and using financial resources in conjunction with all other considerations to provide better services. It is true that central control can also discourage managers from mismanaging, but there are times and other circumstances in which a subtler balance between the control of inputs and outputs might produce better services. One theme has been to have a broad control of inputs and outputs at the centre, but devolve detailed controls to budgetholders.

The individual elements of central financial control have potential weaknesses that are easily identified. The non-hypothecation of taxes, in separating the right of taxpayers to receive particular services from their duty to pay taxes, while it is fundamental to the nature of government, can be said to miss out on opportunities to increase taxes. At some times, for some services, taxpayers may be unwilling to pay higher general taxes but willing to pay a particular tax, as long as the proceeds are restricted to a particular service. Such a willingness is often expressed only hypothetically (perhaps in answer to a questionnaire that asks, 'Would you be willing?'), but it does recur. This is an approximation of the personal choices for private goods and services that underpin markets. In the typical cases of governments with limited means, such opportunities are hard to resist, but they do weaken central control.

The gross budget principle can be said to discourage budgetholders from identifying additional sources of revenue. If the revenue is, as it were, lost to the centre (which perhaps will decide to use it to increase another service's budget), the budgetholder has no incentive to search for it. There are various ways in which the principle can be modified to provide such an incentive. The centre can agree with the budgetholder in advance that a percentage or amount of the extra revenues can be spent in any legitimate way by them, with the balance reverting to the centre. This agreement might authorise the specific forms of the revenues or be a general licence to collect whatever additional revenues they can. The principle can also be abandoned (for specific forms of finance or generally) so that the revenues remain for the budgetholder to spend.

There are many reasons for it being improper to provide such incentives from the point of view of the government as a whole, as reluctant as that government might be to risk foregoing the additional revenues. The ability of one budgetholder to collect money from a group of service recipients, narrowly or broadly defined, who are rich and very willing to pay so long as their neighbourhood is the prime beneficiary, can fundamentally subvert a government's strategies.

Annuality has one commonplace effect, on the timing of annual spending: a disproportionate amount of spending will take place in the final months of the fiscal year that might otherwise have taken place earlier in the year or in the subsequent year. This effect is so familiar that it has been given a variety of names – 'year end rush' and 'hurry up spending' are two. It also has nicknames, such as 'spring sale' and 'March madness' (when the fiscal year ends on 31 March), 'Christmas season' (when the fiscal year ends on 31 December, perhaps, but also from the point of view of the suppliers or contractors for whom it is 'Christmas' in that they are the immediate beneficiaries of the spending) and, more specifically, 'grand piano syndrome', meaning that a keyboard might have been a more efficient, if less grand, purchase. These names at least imply, even when they are not explicit, that the timing of the spending (which, without annuality, would seem odd) causes the spending to be wasteful, uneconomic, inefficient and ineffective and/or of inappropriate quality (usually inappropriately high, extravagant).

How, in more detail, does annuality affect the timing of spending? There is an imperative to not overspend. In an uncertain world in which the annual budget may have been set months (perhaps even years) before the fiscal year, it is natural for budgetholders to want, if possible, to wait until the demands of the financial year are clearer before they spend their budgets. At its most innocuous, it is simply the case that the passage of time has reduced the amount of uncertainty. It discourages the practice of dividing a discretionary budget by 12 (months) and smoothing the spending over the year. Instead, it encourages the holding back of, say, half of the annual budget, then spending it in the final quarter. The uncertainty about demands on the annual budget can be exacerbated by the definition of the fiscal year. In countries such as the UK, where the final months are winter months, then spending on roads, for example, can be severely affected by the weather.

If such a budget profile were planned and executed as planned, it would be unfair to judge this disproportionate spending as a 'rush' of spending. Rather, it is a rational way to deal with uncertainty, given the imperative to not overspend the annual budget. Moreover, for some kinds of capital spending there can be a systematic factor that leads to disproportionate spending in the final quarter, in which the projects require many months, sometimes years, from their initiation to their becoming operational – a lead time that cannot easily be reduced. Such projects include, for example, those that require extensive discussion with the public or pressure groups and involve complex technical stages in their implementation.

It is the imperative to not overspend the budgets, coupled with the uncertainty of demands on it, that leads to disproportionate spending. The other part of the principle of annuality – which requires government departments to not spend less than the budget – is a further, but less strong cause. There are also other causes, somewhat less wholesome, that can easily lead to undesirable spending merely to ensure that budgets are not surrendered to the centre.

One such cause is the budgetholders distinguishing between their own objectives and those of the government as a whole. For example, an underspend that is surrendered to the centre can be seen as a loss to the service for which it was originally allocated. At its extreme, this view challenges the other view that public money is spent in the public interest, as determined by the government as a whole. Instead, the thinking is that, once the budget for a service has been authorised, the money is the budgetholder's money to be spent only on that budgetholder's services. This perception – that some politicians and officers have a stronger association with 'their own' service than with the public interest as a whole – is a common one.

A second cause derives from the centre's interpreting spending against the budget as a signal of the budgetholder's need to spend. This signal is especially strong when there is no systematic profiling of the budget (that is, a formal, agreed pattern of spending the budget over the financial year) and no overt, profiled relationship between spending and outputs and outcomes. Notwithstanding the fact that the authorised annual budget demonstrated the original need to spend, subsequent underspending signals that the authorised budget was not wholly needed and next year's and subsequent years' budgets can be reduced. The signal would be even stronger in cash management systems based on the authorised budget, in which cash is forwarded from the centre to the departments' bank accounts in tranches before, during and after the financial year. If the interim tranches are not spent before further tranches become due, the signal intensifies as not only has a budget been authorised that appears greater than is required, but actual cash has been moved out of the central bank accounts that is not needed.

Using the budget to avoid losing it can produce wasteful and extravagant spending, such as low-priority spending on goods and services and grants to other governments, not-for-profits or for-profits, spending on goods and services of inappropriately high quality and spending on low-quality goods that then languish in storerooms. Suppliers might be put under pressure to fulfil orders, perhaps too quickly. The incentives to use the budget might be so strong that budgetholders resort to manipulating the transactions, colluding with suppliers by making payments to suppliers in the old year while goods and services are delivered in the new or making payments in the old year and refunding them in the new, for example. This can extend to manipulating the accounting against the budget, even to the point of committing fraud.

Because examples of the undesirable effects of annuality are commonplace, there have been continual attempts to counter them. These have focused on tighter systems of control of procurement, remuneration policies that reward budgetholders who underspend and limits being set on the amount that can be spent in the later months of the year.

Better approaches to planning and therefore scheduling spending are probably the most fruitful. Earlier identification in the fiscal year of possible underspendings is important in this, so that budgets can be reallocated. The budgetholders could then develop carefully prepared 'off the shelf' projects that will be efficient and effective, which could be quickly implemented to make use of any underspend. The same idea can be applied to quick discretionary spending on repairs and maintenance, staff training and the acquisition of IT and other equipment.

Of course, rather than address the undesirable effects of annuality, the rule itself can be modified, even abandoned, by, for example, permitting the carrying forward of some percentage, perhaps all, of the unspent balances to the next fiscal year. It is important to realise that such a modification only addresses one part of the problem: it endorses the underspending in the current year, but does not prevent the centre using this as a signal to cut future budgets. There have, however, been cases of this being implemented.

It could even be argued, by extension, that the other aspect of annuality be abandoned – that is, not only could underspendings be carried forward but also overspendings. In more direct terms, budgets could be overspent. This would certainly strike at the heart of the financial control system. The problem with it, to say the least, is that it is much harder to persuade budgetholders to make a necessary reduction in next year's spending (to cover the overspending in this year's) than it is to persuade them to increase next year's spending (to use up the underspending).

Detailed specification of budgets can be undesirable. Its premise is that the centre knows better than the budgetholders what their budgets should buy, which, in large governments, is unlikely. In addition, budgetholders can build up hidden reserves in line items that do not attract political attention (by overestimating the required amounts) and subsequently move them into line items that otherwise would. Virement rules can mitigate the effects of this, but these are applied during the fiscal year and political attention might not be as high then as it is during the budget authorisation period.

6.3 Budget reporting

However the budget is generated, in whichever form and whether within a centralised or devolved control setting, accounting uses records of transactions to compare the actual position with the budgeted position and reports on the findings of that comparison. For external financial reporting, the reporting is usually annual, at high levels of aggregation for the government as a whole and its characteristics determined by GAAP, but the integrity of this external control depends on the quality of the internal reporting system. Issues for these internal reports are:

- timeliness
- amount of detail
- understandability
- controllability
- profiling
- accounting basis.

On timeliness and the level of detail, ICT offers the technical possibility of reporting everything in real time. At low levels of managerial responsibility, for control of large numbers of individual transactions, this will be necessary. Higher levels of responsibility, however, will tend to need higher levels of aggregation in the reporting. This trade-off is affected by an important technical accounting issue.

As the accounting widens its concerns from individual transactions to aggregating and measuring costs, for example, the more difficult that accounting becomes. Allocating costs over time (depreciation, for example) and allocating costs through space (such as support services) is ever more difficult as the period of time shortens. Monthly reporting will be typical for many levels within an organisation, but even this can create technical accounting problems.

A very practical problem, but a very common one, relates to the understandability of control reports. As mundane as this might seem, as it might appear that any system can easily be made understandable, the problem recurs because of the different perceptions of the controllers and the controlled. The level of accounting sophistication can vary between the two groups from high to none, given that, for many budgetholders, the skills of budgetholding are ancillary to their specialisms. As well as being sophisticated, however, accounting can be blind to the needs of non-accountants – as any profession can. For example, this can be apparent in its use of jargon, which in accounting's case has a disproportionate number of inconsistent terms. When the controllers design the control reports, as they often will, the needs of the controlled require special consideration.

The logic of rational budgetary control is that each budgetholder is able to control the relevant budget. In reality, controllability is very complex. The fundamental questions of supply and demand for public services and the causes and effects of spending cannot be determined by budgetary control systems, but the reporting is important to them. Within narrow ranges of understanding of control, there are different forms and extents of it. An employees budget is different from a supplies budget, for example. The budgetholder may have little month-to-month control of the number of employees or their salaries, but the control is not zero – not discouraging staff from leaving and not rushing to fill vacant posts are important forms of control. The supplies budget may seem to be at the budgetholder's daily discretion, in that orders can be issued quickly, but the demand for those supplies might be so direct and incontrovertible that there is no effective control: the supplies have to be bought. There may also be no discretion over the choice of supplier, perhaps because the government has one procurement process that has to be followed, and so the quality and price of the supplies are outside the budgetholder's control.

In a similar vein, significant parts of a budget may not be under the effective control of the budgetholder because other staff within the ambit of the budget are causing costs to be incurred. Thus, the financial transactions are initiated and fulfilled by the budgetholder, but they are caused by service specialists who are providing their services without holding budgets directly. Clinicians, who are not budgetholders, have the 'clinical freedom' to admit patients to, and treat them in, hospitals; professors, who are not budgetholders, have the 'academic freedom' to admit students and establish degree programmes of teaching and learning; police officers, who are not budgetholders, have the law enforcement powers to make arrests and prosecute offenders. Adding a budget to each service specialist, with the concomitant education and training in managing budgets that this requires, is a recurring theme in attempts to address this issue.

As the records of transactions are central to budgetary reporting, the controllability of the actual recording of them is of interest. For internal financial control purposes, the initial stages of transactions will be segregated from the final stages of processing and paying invoices, which will take place within a technical accounting department. From the point of view of the budgetholders, their lack of control over some of the data in budgetary reports, which are being used to control their behaviour, can be contentious. From the point of view of the controllers, their lack of control can invite manipulation of the data. The accounting basis has an important role to play in addressing these points of view.

The different extents of control that necessarily subsist can be perceived differently by the controllers and the controlled. When the controllers have more of the power – perhaps because resources are especially scarce – a tight budget might be used to force a budgetholder to take more control, perhaps by forcing the budgetholder to make what might otherwise be judged unreasonable decisions.

Budgetary control is ultimately control of the annual budget. Control of spending within the year is better when the annual budget is profiled. The budget profile is the planned pattern of spending over the year. A monthly profile predicts the proportion of spending in each consecutive month and the actual spending in each month is compared with this profile. For some large line items, the profile will be of even spending over the year, such as for salaries and wages typically in twelfths. There will, however, often be line items that have other patterns. Sometimes they are easily discernible (seasonal, for example), sometimes not. The size of these may warrant analysing and modelling past data to determine them. There may be line items that cannot be profiled, for which a default profile will be to assume that the budget is spent in twelfths.

Budget profiling is only a prediction, however sophisticated the basis is. The control of actual spending against the profile is not control against an absolute, in the way that ultimate control against the annual budget might be taken to be. The reporting system represents the profile as an absolute, but the practice of control also uses the actual monthly spending to test the quality of the predictions.

Exhibit 6.1 is an example of a budgetary control report for the first six months of the year.

Exhibit 6.1 **Budgetary control report for gross expenditure for the Social Services Department, City of Eutopia, for the half year ended [*date*] 20x2**

£000	Annual budget	Budget profile: budget to date	Actual spending to date	Under- (over-) spending against profile	Balance remaining of annual budget
[1]	[2]	[3]	[4]	[5]	[6]
Employees					
Salaries	11,040	5,500	5,500	–	5,540
Payroll taxes	630	300	300	–	330
Pension contributions	1,280	600	600	–	680
Wages	1,750	850	800	50	950
Payroll taxes	30	15	10	5	20
Pension contributions	120	60	55	5	65
Premises					
Heating and lighting	800	600	450	150	350
Transport					
Fuel	300	100	120	(20)	180
Supplies					
Materials	300	50	130	(80)	170
Total	16,250	8,075	7,965	110	8,285

Department A Budgetary Control Report
6 months ended [*date*], 20x2

Column 3 is the profile of the annual budget, showing expected spending to date. Some of the line items are expected to be approximately a half of the annual budget but others show proportions significantly different from a half. Column 3 is then compared with actual spending at the end of the first half year (Column 4) to reveal the resultant under- or overspending (Column 5). Column 6 reminds the budgetholder that ultimate control is against the annual budget.

Ideally the periodic budgetary control reports should include commitments and an accrual basis, so that a complete picture of the financial position to date is provided (cash-based systems are of limited effectiveness for budgetary control purposes).

Budgetary control is not just about trying to ensure that budgets are not over- or underspent; it is also about monitoring so that the controllers can take action, other than with the budgetholder, to address variances. For example, supplementary budgets might be needed within the year.

FURTHER READING

Bromwich, M. and Lapsley, I. (1997) 'Decentralisation and management accounting in central government', *Financial Accountability and Management*, 12(2): 181–201.

Hyndman, N., Jones, R. and Pendlebury, M. (2007) 'An exploratory study of annuality in the UK public sector', *Financial Accountability and Management*, 23(2): 215–37.

Jones, R. (2001) 'Management accounting in government: resurrecting the classic rules of budget theory', *The Irish Accounting Review*, 8(2): 45–68.

Chapter 7

Costing

The foundation of costing techniques lies in for-profit manufacturing organisations, in which the original purpose of the techniques was to cost individual, physically identifiable products for sale. The techniques have since been extended to apply to service organisations, including not-for-profits. In governments, costing techniques are less extensively used than they are in for-profits but, when they are used, they can be very important to managers, politicians, service recipients and taxpayers – sometimes controversially so. Which particular techniques are used depends on the purposes of the costing – whether it is for organisational units, programmes and products, pricing and reimbursement, incremental changes in output or for outsourcing, for example.

7.1 Organisational units, programmes and products

Knowing the causal relationships between measures of inputs and outputs is the foundation of costing: how do costs vary with output? Costing is most useful and clearest when the outcomes are closely associated with the outputs and the outputs are physically identifiable products for sale, as in a traditional manufacturing business. It is clearest in such a situation because a significant proportion of the organisation's costs will relate directly (direct costs) with the fundamental purpose of the organisation, to make the products.

These are sometimes called the engineered costs, to emphasise that the labour, machinery and materials required by the existing production process within the land and buildings, and their costs, are matters of physical engineering and thereby traced by the accounting records. These direct costs can also be classified as variable, semi-variable and fixed. Variable costs vary directly with changes in the level of output and fixed costs are not affected by changes in the level of output, while semi-variable costs are partly fixed and partly vary with changes in the level of output.

Costing is at its most useful here because these direct costs can naturally be matched with the selling prices. The causal relationships are significant to the organisation as a whole, are strong and, because inputs and outputs are measured on the same money scale, at the heart of the management of a for-profit organisation.

The organisation will incur costs other than engineered costs. These are costs that do not relate directly (indirect costs or overheads) to the products that are made. They may be incurred in a department in which the products are made or in other, support departments. These are sometimes called the discretionary costs. They are discretionary in the sense that, because they are mostly fixed and do not vary directly with the products made, it is at the organisation's discretion to vary them without clearly affecting the products made. The causal relationships of these inputs to outputs are not completely clear, though, for some parts of the inputs, they will be clearer than others. This is reminiscent of the telling old epigram, 'We know that half of the marketing budget is wasted – we just don't know which half'.

There are different reasons for cost accountants needing – despite the lack of clarity – to allocate all these costs of the organisation to the products (the term 'allocation' signals that the allocations are essentially artificial, however sensitive they are in terms of representing the causality). The logic behind this 'full costing' is that, once the outputs of the organisation are defined (within an agreed set of outcomes, stated or unstated), they must have caused all the organisation's costs to have been incurred, otherwise they would not, and should not, have been incurred.

The general purpose financial reports of the organisation must include total costs of the organisation, of course, so, when inventories of incomplete and final products are included in the balance sheet, they are fully costed. In the same way, full costing is required when individual products are being priced by the costing system or, as a comparator, when they are priced, in effect, by the market. When an organisation's list of products made is exhaustive, its total costs must be recovered by those products. There are a few traditional volume bases available to allocate such costs, supplemented now by substantial experience with bases suggested by activity-based costing.

Understanding the cost structure – the relationship between variable and fixed costs – is relevant for decisions about incremental (or decremental) changes in the volume of products made at the margin of the existing volume. How do costs vary with output within manageable increases or decreases in current production (known as the relevant range)? The technique for understanding this is cost–volume–profit analysis. It identifies that part of the cost structure – the fixed costs – in which costs do not vary with output and those that vary continuously – the variable costs. Within a narrow relevant range, this distinction is enough, but the analysis is always aware (in the background as it were) of costs that do vary, but not continuously – in discrete steps, for example. The proportion of variable costs to fixed costs varies by business and industry. The analysis is of full costs, but the emphasis is on the variable costs.

Costing techniques are used for other purposes where full costing would be wrong. The outputs of the organisation caused the total costs. When a change in volume of production is being considered within a relevant range, the focus is on the variable costs. What will happen to costs, though, when, for example, some parts of the production process for a product are outsourced? In such a case, a volume change within a relevant range is not being made, but a discrete chunk of the costs of production are being extracted from the organisation. The focus is now on those parts of the full costs that will *not* be incurred after they have been outsourced. The distinctions between direct and indirect and variable and fixed within the relevant range might help, but will not necessarily determine the costs that will be saved.

These costing techniques are used in definitive parts of governments, to know the causal relationships between inputs, outputs and outcomes. They are of more limited use in such situations than they are in for-profit organisations, for which they were originally developed – for three reasons. First, they do not deal with outcomes. Outcomes are much less easily collapsed into measurable outputs in governments. Second, variable costs are a much smaller proportion of a government's costs than they are in a for-profit organisation making physically identifiable products, and may even be zero. There may be situations in which there are no costs that clearly vary with a measurable output. Third, there are no revenues from the measurable outputs to match with any variable costs. The causal relationships that the costing techniques address are less significant to the organisation as a whole, less strong and, because inputs and outputs are not measured on the same money scale, less important to the management of the government. The techniques are demanded, however, and the information they provide is highly valued, so is continually contested. In notable contexts, they are so contestable that the typically unregulated management accounting becomes regulated, with costing rules being imposed on the organisation by external bodies (such as funders of all kinds, professional accounting bodies and the Cost Accounting Standards Board within the US Office of Federal Procurement Policy).

The main ways in which they are used in governments are in allocating costs to organisational units, programmes and products, costing for pricing and reimbursement, costing incremental changes in output and outsourcing.

For organisational units, programmes and products, the essential costing technique is the allocation of indirect costs for full costing. For organisational units, the bookkeeping records the direct costs of each department and sub-unit. Most of these organisational units provide services directly to external service recipients, sometimes known as line departments. Some of the units, however, only provide support services internally to the line departments. The direct costs of these support services are allocated to the line departments.

When, additionally there is a programme structure, the essence is the same. The organisation's bookkeeping simultaneously identifies the direct costs of each programme and the costing allocates the remaining indirect costs to each programme. For both organisational units and programmes, the accounting basis can properly be on a cash, an accrual or a mixed basis.

For products, the typical context is one in which the organisational structure collects the direct and indirect costs of the organisational units and the full costs are then traced to products. When the relationship between the organisational structure and the programmes is not strong, so that the organisational structure is orientated more towards inputs, the need for a product focus is the greater. The costing of products can also be in a context in which the programme structure collects the direct and indirect costs, which are then traced to products. The rationale of the programme structure – in emphasising outputs and outcomes – suggests a more natural link to the costing of products.

The accounting basis for the costing of products cannot sensibly be a cash basis. It has to be an accrual basis that extracts the operating costs from the total costs and uses those operating costs to approximate economic costs. The information on the budget needed for each product, whether a cash- or obligation-based budget, can be derived from those budgets. The accrual-based cost of the service provided is in addition, but it is the only useful basis for product costing.

The essential costing issues involved can be reduced to two. First, the indirect costs are allocated to the line departments or programmes. Second, the full costs of the line departments or programmes are allocated to the products. The following examples refer to line departments (but their essence is retained if these are changed to programmes).

The typical kinds of indirect costs are office costs. The ones that would apply whatever the accounting basis are the operating costs of buildings, equipment and employees (the capital costs of land and buildings would only be relevant under cash bases). The chain of causal relationships is weaker in some places than in others – that is, the relationship between outcomes and outputs can be weak; that between high-level outputs and low-level outputs stronger; that between low-level outputs and direct costs strong; between low-level outputs and indirect costs weak.

In line item budgeting for organisational structures that do not have output measurement, the allocation of indirect costs uses input bases. The simplest ones are floor space for building costs and the number of employees for employee costs. When the line departments are in the same building as the support departments, the relative percentage of floor space might be more acceptable than if they are in separate buildings (why would the physical size of a line department represent support building costs incurred?). The number of employees the line department has might be an acceptable representation of the use made of support employees. The representations are tenuous, necessarily so, but simple to measure. This is the first stage in the allocation of indirect costs.

The second stage introduces the outputs of the line departments: products. The full costs of the line departments are related to those products, to calculate the costs per product. This is most easily done when there is only one product per line department. When there are multiple products per line department, there are the same problems of identifying the direct costs per product and then allocating the indirect costs per product.

These two separate stages have parallels in the for-profit traditional manufacturing organisation. The first stage allocates the indirect costs of the support units to a production unit, using an arbitrary basis, such as floor area or number of employees, and the second stage absorbs the indirect costs that have been allocated to the production department, plus the production department's own indirect costs, into the products that are being produced using a volume of input basis (direct labour hours or direct machine hours are two common examples). Activity-based costing challenges the relevance of allocating costs on a volume of input basis and, instead, attempts to trace indirect costs to products by identifying the activities that drive costs. It essentially points out that what matters is how the elements required (the activities carried out) to make the product incur support costs. The causal relationships are still difficult to establish, by the definition of indirect costs, but by trying to establish a direct connection between products and support costs, by missing out the focus on the production department itself, activity-based costing can provide representations of causality that are more sensitive. The insights of activity-based costing can similarly improve the costing in the governmental case. By concentrating on the direct connection between products and support costs and missing out the focus on the line department as an organisational unit more sensitive representations of the causality can be identified.

Exhibit 7.1 provides an example of the conventional method of allocating the indirect costs of support departments. Exhibit 7.2 develops the example given in Exhibit 7.1 to use an activity costing basis.

The costs per client using the activity basis are lower for Subunit 1 and higher for Subunit 2 than with the conventional method. The argument of the activity basis is that, in attempting to identify drivers of costs, these provide a better approximation of causal relationships than the conventional method. The sophistication of the method could be increased by studying the extent to which different types of clients affect the support services provided by Subunit 3. For example, if a study revealed that the clients of Subunit 2 require twice the level of support from Subunit 3 than the clients of Subunit 1 do, then the allocation could reflect this by weighting the allocation to Subunit 2 by a factor of 2, as in Exhibit 7.3.

This results in different costs per client and, although it may give a better estimate than before of full cost, the costs of collecting the data have to be considered when judging whether or not the increased sophistication is justified. If the study of drivers is inexpensive to carry out and the results reasonably stable over time, the sophistication may be justified. If, instead, the results are not

Exhibit 7.1 Allocation of indirect costs from support departments to and within Unit A, Social Services Department, City of Eutopia: conventional method

Unit A within the Social Services Department, City of Eutopia has three subunits: Subunit 3 provides support to Subunits 1 and 2 that provide services directly to each of two homogeneous groups of clients. Subunits 1, 2 and 3 are in City Hall and occupy 50, 40 and 10 per cent of the floor space of Unit A. Subunits 1, 2 and 3 have 180, 60 and 40 employees respectively. Subunit 1 provides services to 160 clients and Subunit 2 to 450 clients. The total direct cost of Subunit 3 is £820,000, of which £180,000 is for premises and £640,000 for employees. The direct costs of Subunits 1 and 2 are £2,200,000 and £2,320,000 respectively.

Unit A uses the service of the city's central Legal Department, which occupies rented office space close to City Hall. The Legal Department has 40 employees and incurs total costs of £2,560,000. As well as servicing Unit A, the Legal Department provides services for other departments in the city with a total of 1000 employees.

In allocating the costs of the Legal Department to Unit A and other departments of the city, the employee numbers in each department are used. The total number of employees in Unit A is 280 and in other departments 1000, giving a total of 1280. The allocations for the three subunits in Unit A are as follows: Subunit 1: 180/1280 × £2,560,000 = £360,000; Subunit 2: 60/1280 × £2,560,000 = £120,000; Subunit 3: 40/1280 × £2,560,000 = £80,000.

In allocating the costs of Subunit 3 to Subunits 1 and 2, the premises costs are allocated using the approximate proportion of floor space (Subunit 1: 50/90 × £180,000 = £100,000; Subunit 2: 40/90 × £180,000 = £80,000). The employee costs of Subunit 3, which now consist of the direct costs of £640,000 plus the allocated Legal Department costs of £80,000 (total £720,000), are allocated using the proportion of employees (Subunit 1: 180/240 × £720,000 = £540,000; Subunit 2: 60/240 × £720,000 = £180,000).

£		Unit A		Legal
	Subunit 1	Subunit 2	Subunit 3	Department
Direct costs	2,200,000	2,320,000	820,000	2,560,000
Allocated costs:				
Legal Department	360,000	120,000	80,000	(560,000)
	2,560,000	2,440,000	900,000	2,000,000
Subunit 3 premises	100,000	80,000	(180,000)	–
Subunit 3 employees	540,000	180,000	(720,000)	–
Total net expenditure	£3,200,000	£2,700,000	–	–
Number of clients	160	450	–	–
Cost per client	£20,000	£6,000	–	–

stable and have to be carried out frequently or if the costs of the study are otherwise much higher, then the costs may exceed the benefits of the increased sophistication.

The ability of the accounting system to trace direct costs to organisational units, programmes and products, then allocate indirect costs, is not technically difficult. Especially when there are significant proportions of indirect costs, however, the results are arbitrary and can, therefore, be contested, including by accounting theorists who are uneasy with the arbitrariness. There are many situations, though, in which the costing is demanded variously by managers, politicians, service recipients and taxpayers, and is continually contested. A departmental manager who is a budgetholder will be intensely interested in the central support costs that the costing said the manager caused. Did the manager of Unit A have a choice in incurring these costs? Could the services have been

Exhibit 7.2 Allocation of indirect costs from support departments to and within Unit A, Social Services Department, City of Eutopia: activity costing

The basic data are the same as in Exhibit 7.1. The Legal Department, however, no longer allocates its costs on the basis of numbers of employees in the departments/units of the city that it serves, but on an agreement based on the level of service provided. The charge for the agreed level of service is based on chargeable hours that the Legal Department provides for each department/unit. On this basis, the agreed Legal Department charge to the whole of Unit A does, by coincidence, remain unchanged at £560,000, but the charges to Subunits 1, 2 and 3 change to £105,000, £360,000 and £95,000 respectively.

The costs of Subunit 3, under an activity-based approach, are not allocated to Subunits 1 and 2 on the basis of floor area or numbers of employees, but on the basis of the variable that best drives the costs of Subunit 3. In this case, the driver is the number of clients served by the subunits (Subunit 1: 160/610 × £915,000 = £240,000; Subunit 2: 450/610 × £915,000 = £675,000).

£		Unit A	
	Subunit 1	Subunit 2	Subunit 3
Direct costs	2,200,000	2,320,000	820,000
Legal Department charges	105,000	360,000	95,000
	2,305,000	2,680,000	915,000
Subunit 3 costs	240,000	675,000	(915,000)
Total	£2,545,000	£3,355,000	–
Number of clients	160	450	–
Cost per client	£15,906	£7,456	–

Exhibit 7.3 Allocation of indirect costs from support departments to Social Services Department, City of Eutopia: activity costing

The basic data are the same as in Exhibit 7.2, except that the allocation for Subunit 3 is weighted by an additional factor of 2 to reflect a better measure of the cost driver (Subunit 1: 160/1,060 × £915,000 = £138,000; Subunit 2: 900/1,060 × £915,000 = £777,000). (The allocations have been rounded to the nearest £'000.)

£		Unit A	
	Subunit 1	Subunit 2	Subunit 3
Direct costs	2,200,000	2,320,000	820,000
Legal Department charges	105,000	360,000	95,000
	2,305,000	2,680,000	915,000
Subunit 3 costs	138,000	777,000	(915,000)
Total	£2,443,000	£3,457,000	–
Number of clients	160	450	–
Cost per client	£15,269	£7,682	–

bought elsewhere within the organisation (from the support subunit) or from outside the organisation? Is the amount allocated reasonable given the benefits the unit received? A politician with a pet programme will be intensely interested, if not in the costs said to be incurred, then in the budget allocated to the programme. Is the amount enough? Is the amount allocated reasonable given the amount of control the programme has over the department? For service recipients, who naturally have a pet programme, is the amount enough to satisfy their needs? When the output of a service is increased at the same or lower total cost, to provide fuller use of fixed costs, is the service still reasonable to existing recipients? For taxpayers, the full cost of a department, programme or product is central to decisions about whether each should be paid for, wholly or in part, by others (by charging service recipients, claiming reimbursement from another level of government or outsourcing).

Recurring controversy about central support costs occurs in multifunctional, democratically elected governments in which the debate contrasts the reasonable costs of the services directly provided to service recipients with the costs of democracy. The unallocated costs may be the reasonable costs of democracy. There is a parallel case in not-for-profits. Donors can have a strong feeling, however irrational it may sometimes be, that every penny of their individual donation should be applied directly to service recipients, not to the central support of the not-for-profit. Not-for-profits are forbidden from political activism, but have a natural interest in soliciting general support for their work. If the costs remain unallocated to programmes, the percentage of indirect costs is higher than it would otherwise be, perhaps discouraging donors.

An obvious way to avoid the artificiality and arbitrariness of full costing of support services is to subject the costs to a negotiation of prices between the line departments and the service departments, although if full costing is imperative the negotiations themselves will be artificial.

7.2 Pricing and reimbursement

Though the definitive form of government provides services free at the point of delivery – financed at bottom by taxation – within that form governments also charge for services below and at and above cost. There are several rationales for this:

- it is for the sake of the additional revenues – services are needed, lenders will not lend, taxpayers will not pay more, grants or donations are not available
- the charges do not have to be hypothecated as those charged will pay extra anyway
- the charges can be hypothecated when those charged require it
- it is to ration service provision – by discouraging extravagant or frivolous consumption, encouraging most efficient and effective use and penalising undesirable outcomes
- it is to improve the management because the relationships between input and output are clearer and the outputs provide clear signals of demand
- it is to regulate the demand for services that would otherwise be in the private sector, by creating a government monopoly.

All of these rationales can lead to different prices being charged in relation to costs, including penalties being charged that have no relation to costs. In all cases, however, it is important for accounting to know the full costs that are, or are not, being charged. The charges are ultimately subject to managerial and political decisions, but they are likely to be better when they are based on full cost information.

7.3 Incremental changes in output

The governmental unit's cost structure explains how costs vary with output within manageable increases or decreases in the relevant range. When learning from the for-profit technique of cost–volume–profit analysis, the analysis loses the sales revenue data (and concomitant profit calculations) and becomes cost–volume analysis. It identifies that part of the cost structure – the fixed costs – in which costs do not vary with output and those that vary continuously – variable costs. Within a narrow relevant range, the costs that do vary but not continuously (in discrete steps, for example) can often be ignored.

Cost–volume analysis can either identify the cost structure usefully or not. The technique is not in search of an application. Rather the setting determines when the analysis is useful. In each setting, a decision is being made about incremental changes in the measured output that is used to manage the governmental unit, so the fixed and variable costs of those changes can be robustly identified. This will always be within the wider context of higher-level outputs and outcomes. For the analysis to be useful, it has to harmonise with that context.

Exhibit 7.4 gives the data for a residential home for elderly people. The care provided to each individual client in that group setting is the wider context of the cost–volume analysis. A crude but important output measure used by the manager is the number of places, the number of beds. The manager knows that these categories of output are not homogeneous, that the quality of service is different for each bed – the physical beds and their location matter and may be different and, of course, each resident cannot be assumed to have the same needs. The number of beds is a useful measure nonetheless. The analysis is being used to determine how costs will change as the occupancy rate rises from 80 to 100 per cent, to increase the use of this service. This would be the most efficient

Exhibit 7.4 Residential home for the elderly, Social Services Department, City of Eutopia: cost–volume analysis

The maximum number of beds in this home at any one time is 20. The total annual cost (on the full costing basis) of the home is £332,800, about £6400 a week. At the time of the analysis, there are 16 residents – a bed occupancy rate of 80 per cent.

The cost per resident week is £6400/16 = £400 per resident week.

Fixed costs are £4800 a week and variable costs £1600 a week (£100 per resident week), so taking four more residents will cost an extra £400 a week only. At full occupancy, the total weekly cost of the home would be £6800 (£4800 + £2000). The greater efficiency this creates for the use of the home would be reflected in the revised average cost per resident week of £6800/20 = £340.

The annual budget required would increase from £332,800 to £353,600 (£6800 × 52), but next year's budget is £343,200. If the home is to fill all 20 places, average costs per resident week must fall to £330. The required reduction in costs could be achieved by reducing fixed costs a week from £4800 to £4600 or reducing variable costs from £100 per resident week to £90 or a combination of the two. As an alternative, the manager may decide that the fixed and variable costs should not be reduced, because any reduction would compromise the existing service provided to each resident. The annual fixed costs are to remain at £249,600 and the variable costs per resident week at £100. With the increased budget of £343,200, the home can take two extra residents.

use of the home and there is demand for the extra places from a waiting list of those in need.

The manager uses the actual cost per resident week to compare this home with other homes in Eutopia and other comparable homes in other comparable local governments, as well as with comparable homes in the private sector, to benchmark. The manager knows that the service offered to the home's residents is individual and there is a variety of acceptable ways of providing the service, but the cost per resident week is a useful measure, widely generated and reported publicly.

Cost–volume analysis points out that, while this measure of average cost (per resident week) is useful for some purposes, it is wrong for understanding how costs will change in the relevant range. Taking four more residents a week will not cost an extra £1600 a week; instead, it will cost an extra £400 a week only (the variable costs).

The home is financed from the Social Services Department's budget, which is a line item incremental budget that covers all the other residential homes and is itself mainly financed by a higher-level government grant distributed on the basis of need, measured by subcategories of the population. The cost–volume analysis identifies the additional budget required to use the home most efficiently and provide the service to people in need. Exhibit 7.4 goes on to show what might happen.

In a wholly comparable for-profit residential home, the cost–volume analysis is extended to give a cost–volume–profit analysis (see Exhibit 7.5), with very different implications for the increase in the occupancy rate.

Exhibit 7.5 **For-profit residential home for the elderly, City of Eutopia: cost–volume analysis**

> The home has an identical cost structure to that of the city's home in Exhibit 7.4 and charges each resident £450 a week. At 80 per cent occupancy, annual profits are £41,600 ([£450 × 16 × 52 = £374,400] − £332,800), which is an average of £2600 a resident. If there is demand from four more potential residents, each willing to pay £23,400 a year, the home will earn more profit than an extra £10,000 a year (£2500 × 4). Because of its cost structure, the weekly contribution that each resident makes to fixed costs is £350 (£450 − £100), £18,200 a year, so the additional profit from four more residents is £72,800 a year (£350 × 4 = £1400 a week).

The for-profit homes residents may have been placed by the Social Services Department, however, because it is responsible for ensuring that those residents receive this kind of care. The price (£23,400 per resident per year) may have been negotiated by the Department. It may have been paid for by the same line item, incremental budget, in which case the budget limit (£343,000) would be even more difficult to achieve as only 14 residents could be accommodated by the Social Services Department in the for-profit home.

7.4 Outsourcing

Full costing is used when like-with-like comparisons are made between a service provided by a government and one provided in the private sector, whether for-profit or not-for-profit. When the actual decision is to be made to transfer a service from one to the other, however, the full costs often include costs that are irrelevant to making that outsourcing decision. Costing for the decision is about identifying the costs that are relevant, usually by identifying and extracting those parts of full costs that are irrelevant. The direct/indirect, fixed/variable distinctions will help (direct operating costs will be avoided following the outsourcing), but the focus must be on relevance, although this will be complicated by judgements about relevance in the short-, medium- and long-term. The relevant costs might include new costs, costs that would not have been incurred had the inhouse government provision continued, such as compensation for loss of office or the costs of regulating or monitoring the private sector provision. Moreover, new revenues (perhaps from the sale of land, buildings and equipment) might be relevant.

As ever, this costing is in the context of outcomes. Particular issues in outsourcing might be the possibility of default by the private sector contractor, either because it goes into administration or is made bankrupt or some other reason, rendering it unable or unwilling to continue to provide the service of the required quality. If the government retains the duty to provide the service, subsequent (including perhaps emergency) costs might be even higher.

Exhibit 7.6 gives an example of an outsourcing decision regarding a laundry service in a government hospital in Eutopia.

Exhibit 7.6 Laundry service in a hospital, City of Eutopia: outsourcing decision

The laundry service is carried out partly inhouse and partly by a private sector contractor. The total volume of laundry work that is generated each week averages 210,000 items and, of these, 140,000 items are laundered by the inhouse service, with the balance being laundered by the contractor. The total volume is not expected to change much over the next few years.

The contractor currently charges 9p per article for the 70,000 items that it undertakes each week, but has recently submitted a written quotation stating that, if it were given a contract to undertake all of the laundry work in the hospital, then the economies of scale that this would produce would enable it to reduce its charges to 7.75p per article.

The annual budget for the Laundry service for the year is as follows.

	£
Inhouse costs:	
Salaries:	
Managers	92,400
Launderers	272,600
Casual workers	111,200
Materials and supplies	44,500
Heat, light and water	147,200
Maintenance of equipment	39,300
Total inhouse costs	707,200
Payments to contractor	327,600
Total	1,034,800

An analysis of the budget reveals that the amounts shown for 'Heat, light and water' and 'Maintenance of equipment' are made up of fixed and variable costs as follows.

	£ fixed costs	£ variable costs
Heat, light and water	41,700	105,500
Maintenance of equipment	9,300	30,000

The casual workers are hired as needed to work weekends and evenings and cover absences of permanent employees. Materials and supplies are assumed to vary directly with the level of activity and there is sufficient capacity to undertake all of the laundry work inhouse.

The manager's options are as follows.

	Completely outsourced	Completely inhouse	Existing arrangement
Volume of activity (articles per week)	210,000	210,000	210,000
Annual costs:	£	£	£
Completely outsourced:			
Contract price (210,000 × 7.75p × 52)	846,300	–	–
Completely inhouse:			
Fixed costs	–	416,000	–
Variable costs (210,000 × 4p × 52)	–	436,800	–
Existing arrangement	–	–	1,034,800
Totals	846,300	852,800	1,034,800

The fixed and variable costs for the inhouse unit are as follows.

	£ fixed costs	£ variable costs
Salaries:		
Managers	92,400	–
Launderers	272,600	–
Casual workers	–	111,200
Materials and supplies	–	44,500
Heat, light and water	41,700	105,500
Maintenance of equipment	9,300	30,000
Totals	416,000	291,200

The variable cost per article is 4p (£291,200/140,000/52).

This analysis suggests that the least costly option would be to outsource the laundry completely. The analysis must now identify the costs that are avoidable if it is decided to choose this option. For example, the size and extent of the new contract might require some of the existing management tasks to be redirected to monitoring the contract. Also, it might take time to redeploy the employees, with some of the existing costs continuing in the short run.

This particular example does not include capital costs. The equipment used by the inhouse laundry service could perhaps be sold if the contract was outsourced and the premises redirected for use by other hospital activities. Alternatively, a depressed market for laundry services might mean that the equipment would have only scrap value, with the costs of dismantling it and clearing the premises exceeding its scrap value.

FURTHER READING

Hoque, Z. (2001) *Strategic Management Accounting*, Chandos.
Drury, C. (2009) *Management Accounting for Business*, Cengage Learning.

Chapter 8

Financial reporting

While there is significant overlap between the financial reporting standards for all for-profit and not-for-profit entities, there are distinctive issues in public sector accounting, namely, budgetary reporting, consolidated financial statements and special accrual accounting issues. There are also particular issues relating to policymaking and policymakers' conceptual frameworks.

8.1 Form and content of published financial reports

Financial, and non-financial, information about the planning, execution and monitoring cycle of a government are matters of internal control that are continually made public in myriad ways – sometimes systematically, sometimes spasmodically. Accounting's perspective on financial reporting requires that two publications occur systematically. First, the annual budget is published when it has been authorised – ideally just before, but, in difficult times, just after the beginning of the fiscal year. Second, the audited financial statements are published – ideally soon after the fiscal year. Accounting would also expect these two publications to be uniform, representing the cycle at two definitive points – before execution and after. In many governments, this expectation is not met, when the budget is not seen as a matter of accounting. The accountant's response is for financial reporting to at least reconcile the audited financial statements with the budget.

There are many other financial reports that are produced at different times and with different focuses. Common examples include budget requests (before the final budget authorisation), revised budgets during the fiscal year (when further budget requests are made), within-year budgetary control reports to politicians and performance audit reports. The wealth of published financial information is an inherent part of modern government. Nevertheless, governmental accounting focuses on the particular importance of the annual authorised budget and the annual audited financial statements, in financial reporting.

When compared with for-profits, there are two fundamental differences between them and the financial reporting of governments. First, in governments, the budgets are not private, whereas in the for-profits they usually are. This difference also affects the audited financial statements because those statements fundamentally include budgets, whereas in for-profits (and private non-profits for that matter) they typically do not.

Second, the accounting basis of the budgets and the audited financial statements is not continually contested and, when it is, not in a heightened controversial way. The financial markets in instantly tradable claims on for-profit organisations provide a natural incentive for investors and lenders to care about the for-profits' audited financial statements (and their unaudited interim financial statements) and, by association, for financial analysts and institutional investors actively to understand the reports. Those analysts have generally not extended their interests into publicly contesting the accounting bases of those reports, but, from the very beginning of the existence of the accounting standard-setting bodies in the mid-twentieth century (which originally focused only on for-profits), the management of for-profits has publicly – and often successfully – contested the accounting bases. Indeed, this particular sense of the politicisation of financial reporting in for-profits has long been commonplace.

Neither of these two differences between governmental and for-profit financial reporting would necessarily be relevant to a discussion of governments. What does make them of great relevance is the influence that the accounting standard-setting bodies have. The codified sets of financial reporting rules, which have such significance in the financial markets, are long-standing, substantially subject to due process, detailed, often changed – and are supported by large budgets and technical support staff. They have significant influence in all accounting. Even within for-profit accounting, they can, for example, seem to dominate management accounting and perhaps even do. They also have an influence on government accounting, notwithstanding the two differences.

An underlying aspect of the differences relates to different senses of confidentiality. In the private sector, 'commercial confidentiality' is a catch-all phrase to cover non-publication of information. In government, an equivalent catch-all phrase is 'national security' or just 'security'. There are many more, day-to-day senses in which confidentiality is required in government, however, even as it conflicts with transparency and, for example, concomitant legislation on the freedom of information. Financial reporting mediates these senses of confidentiality.

The form and content of the published version of the annual budget have not been subject to the pressures from the accounting standard-setting bodies that the published audited financial statements have, in part because of the governments that do not see the budget as a matter for accountants. Building on the audited financial statements, accounting requires them to be included in an annual general purpose financial report for the organisation as a whole. The general purpose financial report is thereby seen as being fundamental to internal control as a whole, not only in relation to the annual financial statements. That is because the inputs, measurable outputs and outcomes are integrated and reported on in one document, with management's responsibilities for internal control clearly identified, the responsibilities of those charged with governance clearly identified and the auditor's opinions on the financial statements, as well as the consistency between them and the unaudited parts of the report, clearly identified. The whole report is prefaced by a report from management, which in the USA is known as 'management's discussion and analysis'. This might include matters such as a formal description of the organisation and its structure, strategic and operational plans and results, an overview of the audited financial statements and risks, relevant uncertainties and trends.

These general purpose financial reports may not include much discussion or reporting of budgets. While this is typical of such financial reports for for-profits, on the general ground of commercial confidentiality, in governments it significantly reduces the relevance of the reports.

Another effect of the fact that the form and content of the published version of the annual budget have not been subject to the pressures the accounting standard-setting bodies have brought to bear in the private sector is that budgets are less uniform. No doubt there are jurisdictions within which these matters are made uniform, but it is probably much more common for each governmental organisation to determine whether or not the budget is published as line items following the organisational structure or as programmes or both (with or without reconciliations), the amount of detail (including the details of capital projects) and the extent to which outputs and outcomes are included.

In incremental budgets, the detailing of the increment can vary significantly. An undeniable accounting question relates to whether or not the budgets include any reference to actuals. In practice, this amounts to whether or not the annual budget for 20x2 – using the budget for 20x1 as its base – should include details of the actuals for 20x0. The basic argument for inclusion is that those actuals provide the budgets (aspirations, hopes) with an anchor to what actually happened. The basic argument against is that the anchor is two years out of date in the minds of budgeters, spending departments, politicians and the public, all of whom are focusing on 20x2. A practical complication to these basic arguments is that the only strict relevance of the 20x0 actuals is when they are compared with the 20x0 budget. The logic of this complication suggests another set of numbers (see Exhibit 8.1), which are a further year out of date.

Exhibit 8.1 Annual budget column headings for the City of Eutopia, for fiscal year 20x2, with budget 20x0

£000	Budget 20x0	Actual 20x0	Original budget 20x1	Revised budget 20x1	Budget 20x2

When the actuals for 20x0 are published, accounting's concern is with reconciling the form and content of those actuals with the published financial statements for 20x0.

The form and content of the published audited financial statements, particularly having been the subject of pressures from accounting's standard-setting bodies, are more homogeneous than those of the published budgets, even if there remains scope for great differences between financial statements. An important element of the difference relates to the different accounting bases that can be adopted.

The integrity of the published financial statements depends, at least, on the accuracy and comprehensiveness of the underlying records of transactions, which are fundamental to the internal control of the organisation. This accuracy and comprehensiveness is demonstrated at least annually when the trial balance is prepared and the annual accounts closed. Without this integrity, no approach to accounting policymaking, however optimal, can rescue the financial statements from being meaningless. The records are the responsibility of the management and are the primary focus of the auditors. Despite their importance, however, financial reporting on the integrity of the records is often only tacit and, even when it is explicit, it can be hard to find. Indeed, as fundamental as the records' integrity is, the question remains as to how best to report on it.

Addressing this question involves extricating the question from questions about external decision-usefulness. This is not easy to do. The reason for this is that we have even less evidence of how governmental financial reports are used externally, and by whom, than we have in for-profits. The word 'stewardship' is often used in this regard. It draws on a centuries-old, and now largely archaic, meaning of 'steward', as someone who has a direct, personal responsibility to account for the money and other resources due to the owner, because the owner entrusted the steward with the right to collect those resources. Stewardship may have included wider responsibilities for the effectiveness of collecting the resources due from others, and for the economy, efficiency and effectiveness of the subsequent use of those resources, but the core meaning that is being drawn on for our purposes is the integrity, the honesty of the steward, represented by the accuracy and comprehensiveness of the steward's personal account. This form of accounting is manifested in many centuries of translated, transcribed and published financial statements, which we know as charge/discharge accounting.

This sense of stewardship can be reported on, in principle and in practice, in many ways. A simple statement from management would suffice, stating that the records are accurate and comprehensive or in accordance with that part of the law which requires them to be, accompanied by an auditor's explicit opinion or even a statement from the auditors that they have no reason to give an opinion because they concur with the statement. A radical alternative would be for such a statement to be accompanied by giving access to the records of every transaction – a possibility that appears increasingly promised by the information revolution. In this narrow sense of stewardship, the access would not be for the purpose of generating decision-useful information, but to provide the possibility of checking that the information is accurate and complete. In practice, the auditors' opinion about fair presentation of the financial statements and conformity with the law, and conformity with budgets, subsume any detailed reference to the integrity of the records. It is important to remember this indispensable aspect of internal control, not least because the integrity of the records is the concern of most accountants, most of the time.

However the records of transaction are reported on, the primary financial report of a government is that of the execution of the budget – that is, the budgetary accounting. Three sets of financial numbers are typically reported on:

- the original authorised budget
- any authorised revised budget
- the comparable actuals.

Beyond that, the form of the accounting is naturally determined by the form of the authorised budgets as those who authorised the budget in a particular form would require the actuals to take the same form. From the accountants' point of view, the requirements of control dictate that the reporting should be determined, at least, by that form of the budget that was actually used during the year to impose control. Accounting would, therefore, typically expect the budgetary accounting to follow the organisational structure and line items. Exhibit 8.2 is a typical example. This could be on a cash or accrual basis but, if it were on a full accrual budgeting and accounting basis, it would take the form of an accrual-based operating statement.

An explanation of differences between the budget and actuals can take different forms. To be comprehensive, there would be explanations of the differences between the actuals and each of the two budgets – the original and the revised. If there is only to be one – on the ground of readability of the report – the comparison with the original budget is the more important as the annual cycle of control starts with the original and ends with the actuals, these points being definitive. The budget to actual explanations could be for each line item or a summary of the significant elements of each departmental unit, for example, or the budget as a whole.

If output measures are inherent in the budgets, the budgetary accounting would naturally include the corresponding actuals. Accounting would want these measures, as far as sensible, to be explicitly related to the financial actuals, but, in any case, would want any financial measures to be derived from, and reconcilable to (even if not publicly so), the budgetary accounting. Exhibit 8.3 provides an example, based on Exhibit 5.13.

Exhibit 8.2 **Budgetary accounting for the City of Eutopia, for the year ended [*date*] 20x2**

£000	Original budget 20x2	Revised budget 20x2	Actual 20x2	Difference between original and actual: under (over)
	City of Eutopia Budget Year ended [*date*], 20x2			
Gross expenditure				
Employees	68,700	69,200	70,100	(1,400)
Premises	10,380	10,100	10,050	330
Transport	5,600	4,900	4,900	700
Supplies	1,570	1,380	1,300	270
Interest	2,400	1,980	1,980	420
Total gross expenditure	88,650	87,560	88,330	320
Gross revenues				
Taxes	37,900	36,500	36,100	1,800
Grants	33,000	35,050	36,000	(3,000)
Donations	3,000	2,100	2,800	200
Charges for services	14,750	15,750	16,800	(2,050)
Total gross revenues	88,650	89,400	91,700	(3,050)
Total government net expenditure	–	(1,840)	(3,370)	(2,730)

Exhibit 8.3 **Output measures added to the budgetary accounting for secondary schools, Education Department, City of Eutopia, year ended [*date*] 20x2, based on Exhibit 5.13**

	Actual 20x1	Original budget 20x2	Actual 20x2
	Education Department, City of Eutopia Budget Year ended [*date*], 20x2		
Cost per student	£4,900	£5,100	£5,500
Cost per thousand population	£910	£950	£970
14-year-olds:			
English:			
A	68%	70%	70%
B	20%	20%	20%
C	12%	10%	10%
Mathematics:			
A	63%	65%	65%
B	20%	25%	26%
C	17%	10%	9%
Science:			
A	77%	80%	81%
B	18%	15%	15%
C	5%	5%	4%
16-year-olds:			
5 or more A or B Grades	44%	45%	46%

Budgetary accounting, which can be called an operating statement, may substantively be the extent of the financial reporting. This would typically be so with cash-based budgetary accounting. Of course, such accounting would produce a balance sheet, but, as it is limited to monetary assets and liabilities, with no other link with the budgetary accounting, this would add little to it. What opens financial reporting up to other forms of accounting – to the financial statements – is the adoption of an accrual accounting base.

Governments have typically addressed accrual accounting in two stages. The first is the publication of the accrual-based financial statements. The second, which has been much less likely to be adopted, is to adopt accrual-based budgeting, either in addition to the cash-based budgetary accounting or as a replacement for it. In both stages, in practice, it has been much more common to adopt ad hoc elements of accrual accounting rather than a comprehensive, cohesive accrual accounting methodology.

The accrual-based financial statements are the conventional ones of for-profit and non-profit organisations. The revenues, expenses, assets and liabilities that accrual accounting recognises are reported in the operating statement and balance sheet, without reference to budgets, as in Exhibits 8.4 and 8.5.

These financial statements add to budgetary accounting's relevant information about the government. Most fundamentally, they add reliable economic measures of the net cost of the services provided, assets and liabilities of the government.

Exhibit 8.4 Operating statement for the City of Eutopia, for the year ended [*date*] 20x2

	20x2	20x1
City of Eutopia Operating Statement Year ended [*date of financial statements*], 20x2	£000	£000
Operating revenue		
Taxes	36,100	33,460
Grants	36,000	27,070
Donations	2,800	2,650
Charges	16,800	13,330
Total operating revenue	91,700	76,510
Operating expenses		
Employees	70,100	63,590
Premises	10,050	7,980
Transport	4,900	4,420
Supplies	1,300	1,200
Total operating expenses	86,350	77,190
Surplus (deficit) from operating activities	5,350	(680)
Finance costs	(1,980)	(1,850)
Gains on sale of equipment	1,360	–
Total non-operating revenue (expense)	(620)	(1,850)
Net surplus (deficit) before extraordinary items	4,730	(2,530)
Extraordinary items	1,340	–
Net surplus (deficit) for the year	3,390	(2,530)

Exhibit 8.5 Balance sheet for the City of Eutopia, at year ended [*date*] 20x2

City of Eutopia
Statement of Financial Position
at [*date of financial statements*], 20x2

	20x2	20x1
	£000	£000
ASSETS		
Current assets		
Cash and cash equivalents	940	360
Receivables	9,700	6,510
Inventories	350	270
Prepayments	1,300	1,100
Investments	3,700	4,600
Total current assets	15,990	12,840
Non-current assets		
Receivables	780	900
Investments	18,250	16,900
Other financial assets	2,800	2,750
Infrastructure, plant and equipment	53,680	52,950
Land and buildings	24,630	22,340
Total non-current assets	100,140	95,840
Total assets	116,130	108,680
LIABILITIES		
Current liabilities		
Payables	8,150	7,050
Short-term borrowing	1,430	1,120
Current portion of long-term borrowing	950	870
Provisions	780	730
Total current liabilities	11,310	9,770
Non-current liabilities		
Payables	1,350	1,860
Long-term borrowing	43,800	40,350
Provisions	680	570
Total non-current liabilities	45,830	42,780
Total liabilities	57,140	52,550
Total net assets	58,990	56,130
NET ASSETS		
Capital contributed by the government	–	–
Reserves	53,680	54,210
Accumulated surpluses (deficits)	5,310	1,920
Total net assets	58,990	56,130

When the financial statements include a partial recognition of unrealised gains and losses (in otherwise historic cost accounting), there might be a statement of these gains and losses. Given that the accrual-based accounting de-emphasises underlying cash flows, there would also be a cash flow statement, ideally using the direct method, to report on those cash flows. Exhibit 8.6 gives an example, based on Exhibits 8.4 and 8.5.

Exhibit 8.6 Cash flow statement for the City of Eutopia, for the year ended [*date*] 20x2

	20x2	20x1
	£000	£000
CASH FLOWS FROM OPERATING ACTIVITIES		
Receipts		
Taxes	36,100	33,460
Grants	36,000	27,070
Donations	2,800	2,650
Charges	15,300	13,110
Total operating receipts	90,200	76,290
Payments		
Employees	(70,100)	(63,590)
Premises	(10,210)	(6,920)
Transport	(6,100)	(2,970)
Supplies	(570)	(1,100)
Interest paid	(1,980)	(1,850)
Total operating payments	(88,960)	(76,430)
Net cash flow from operating activities	1,240	(140)
CASH FLOWS FROM INVESTING ACTIVITIES		
Purchase of infrastructure, plant and equipment	(2,180)	–
Purchase of land and buildings	(2,290)	(1,320)
Purchase of investments and other financial assets	(1,480)	(690)
Proceeds from sale of equipment	1,450	–
Net cash flows from investing activities	(4,500)	(2,010)
CASH FLOWS FROM FINANCING ACTIVITIES		
Proceeds from borrowing	35,850	32,780
Repayment of borrowing	(32,010)	(31,980)
Net cash flows from financing activities	3,840	800
Net increase (decrease) in cash and cash equivalents	580	(1,350)
Cash and cash equivalents, beginning of year	360	1,710
Cash and cash equivalents, end of year	940	360

City of Eutopia
Cash Flow Statement
Year ended [*date of financial statements*], 20x2

Although typical budgetary accounting is cash-based, the cash flow statement adds a synopsis of the cash inflows and outflows that is traditional. The accountant's sense of the cycle of control would be to include budgeted cash flow statements in the financial reporting in addition to these statements of actual cash flows.

8.2 Accrual accounting: special topics

There are special issues for accrual accounting that are still in the early stages of development in governments. Individual sets of accounting standards have developed practical solutions, but these will continue to be improved. One of them relates to consolidated financial statements. There is long-standing and global consensus about the need for consolidations in for-profit financial reporting, but in government financial reporting, the topic has special dimensions and there is much less consensus about the need for consolidations in this case. There are other topics that do not apply to for-profit accounting and have therefore not been subject to standard-setting for very long – heritage assets, infrastructure assets and non-exchange transactions, for example.

In the for-profit context, the external decision-usefulness criterion dominates and, within it, the decision-usefulness of information to investors subsumes the consideration of decisions by any other presumed set of external users – that is, if the needs of investors are satisfied, it is asserted, the needs of all other users will be. Though this assertion can be easily contested, it does at least reflect the clear economic incentive that investors have to understand financial reports, which contrasts with the less strong, or even absence of, economic incentives of other users. Investors in a group of companies need to understand the risk and returns for the group as a whole, and consolidated financial statements are the financial reporting means to achieving this end.

The economic incentives for investors in government to use financial reporting in this way are far less clear and, when they are clear – as in the case of investment in a government that is explicitly not default-free – they usually only relate to the narrow purposes of the investment, not to the government as a whole. If an investor buys a bond issued by a local government to build a road, secured on the tolls collected from the road users, a consolidated financial statement of that local government is of less interest than a financial statement for the road. The need for consolidated financial statements in government is less firmly grounded than it is with for-profits.

There are three different dimensions to consolidated financial statements in government:

- the boundary of the reporting entity
- in a national government, the consolidation of departmental or agency con- solidated financial statements for the government as a whole
- the consolidation of fund accounts in a government as a whole.

The first of these dimensions relates to which entities should be included within the consolidation. It has a close parallel in for-profit accounting, in that the prin- ciple behind the consolidation is not based on ownership or other legal criterion, but on the economic substance of the relations between the organisations, expressed as the extent to which the reporting entity controls the other entities. While there is this parallel, there are also important differences between govern- ments and for-profits. Governments typically have control relationships with a wider variety of kinds of organisations than do for-profits. These can include for- profit organisations, which, at national level can mean state-owned enterprises (similar terms are nationalised industries, public corporations). They can also include private non-profits that, however, receive substantial amounts of public money, but, equally, a wide variety of other organisations that are creations of governments, but not wholly governmental (nor wholly private sector) and otherwise difficult to describe – quasi-autonomous non-governmental organisa- tions (Quangos) is one term for them. Sometimes referred to simply as 'public bodies', the extent and definition of their 'publicness' vary.

More importantly for consolidated financial statements, governments can use a different definition of 'control' than that used in the for-profit context. This is in part necessary because control of a for-profit can usually be expressed in terms of share ownership and the resulting voting power, whereas control of governmental organisations or non-profits often cannot. The UK government, for example, applies a more restrictive sense of control than do for-profits, the effect of which is that significant organisations are excluded from its consolidations. In doing this, it distinguishes between strategic control and control through the government's budget. 'Strategic control' is used to refer to the for-profit concept of control in consolidations. Control through the government's budget is far narrower. It means that, regardless of the amount of strategic control the government has over another organisation, the criterion for including it in the consolidation is only based on the form of control that is expressed through the budget. The UK government's policy is to exclude from the departmental consolidated financial statements those organisations its control of which is limited to this budgetary provision. For example, if the government's budget has a line item that simply provides a large amount of money to the organisation, it will not be consolidated. This would be contentious in a for-profit setting because the size and other significance of the public money might in some circumstances mean significant economic dependence, which would suggest consolidation.

The second dimension of consolidations relates to a national government. In both the UK and the US national governments, each department or agency produces a set of consolidated financial statements. The difficult question then arises of whether or not, and how, these should themselves be consolidated to produce a set of financial statements for the government as a whole. In the USA, there is such a consolidation, known as the government-wide financial statements. In the UK, the consolidation is known as whole-of-government accounts and has been in the law since 2000, but the effective date has not yet been determined.

The complexities of defining the reporting boundary and the influence of government budgeting (referred to above with regard to the first dimension) are naturally greater for a government's financial statements consolidated as a whole than for for-profits because of the larger numbers of organisations it has to consider. In the UK government's case, there is the added issue that the consolidation is to include all local governments. In some countries – especially, but not restricted to, federal states – this can be controversial at the level of constitutional law as local governments may be constitutionally separate from the national government. In all national governments, however, these consolidations have the theoretical and practical problems associated with the fact that the operating statements and balance sheets of each government confront the far longer-standing and more influential 'consolidations' of national government budgeting systems and national accounting. The government budgeting system produces, and thereby 'consolidates', the operating statement of the government as a whole; national accounting does the same for both the operating statement and the balance sheet of the government as a whole. There is no codified set of accounting rules for each government's budget. There is a set for each government's national accounts, but the accounting basis is fundamentally different from the various accounting bases developed by accountants. Reconciliation of the three 'consolidations' appears to be a minimum requirement, but this is neither theoretically nor practically well understood.

Even with reconciliation, the different accounting bases compete with each other and the differences can be used controversially. For example, a government can decide to produce a budget that has a mix of policies – some taken from accounting, some taken from national accounting, some taken from neither. Reconciliation would explain this mix, but the budget numbers – which are the most visible and the most directly influential of the three sets – could still exclude, for example, large amounts of what accounting would book as liabilities. Typical cases are of future unemployment benefits, state pension schemes and the private finance initiative (PFI). Future unemployment benefits and future state pensions might be deemed liabilities, but economics would typically want these matched by future national income, which accounting would not regard as an asset. National accounting might define the reporting boundary for general government such that the PFI contracts signed by governments are judged private, thereby excluding what accounting would more likely judge a huge amount of bookable assets and liabilities. Given the lower status of accounting's views in national governments, compared with those of the budgeters, accounting's policies in the consolidations of the government as a whole can have a peripheral role, in which case the accountant's rational control cycle is fundamentally broken by these heterogeneous sets of accounting bases.

The third dimension of consolidated financial statements in government relates to the consolidation of a set of funds. In this setting, funds are pools of resources that are kept separate, in the accounting system, from the rest of the organisation. This separation does not have to include, and typically does not now include, physical separation of bank accounts. There are a number of reasons for keeping pools of resources separate, the strongest one being because those who are external to the organisation and finance a particular pool require, often legally, such separation. Common examples are of investors and lenders in any kind of organisation, including global agencies such as the World Bank and United Nations, donors in governments and non-profits, including the donations to national and local governments of the larger non-profits termed non-governmental organisations (NGOs), and higher-level governments giving grants, or other transfers, to lower-level governments. There are organisationally different ways to achieve the separation but one way within a given organisation's accounting system is to use funds.

When the use of funds is either required or deemed by the organisation to be required by those who are external to the organisation, a term that is sometimes used to signal this is to state that the fund is restricted, which, in a general sense means that the organisation does not have the discretion to use the fund in any other way. The use of funds may also be required by the other broad category, namely those who are internal to the organisation. Such requirements are naturally not as strong (because the organisation will have greater discretion to change its own requirements) and are sometimes broadly distinguished from restricted funds by calling them 'designated' funds.

The designations take many different forms, with a wide range in the level of force behind them. A government may determine that a tax is to be collected for a sole purpose and collect the tax on that basis. The designation could be so strong that it is effectively a restriction, but it still might be easy to change. An explicit government policy may be to designate a reserve for a sole purpose at some point in the future, which may be difficult to change, but easier than a designated tax. US state and local government accounting includes refined distinctions concerning restrictions and designations.

In complete form, the accounting for each fund produces its own operating statement and balance sheet, so the fund is a self-contained set of accounts and financial statements. For an organisation as a whole, the complete form of fund accounting produces a complete set of these self-contained sets of accounts and financial statements. This financial reporting portrays the organisation as a set of funds, not as one set of consolidated financial statements.

The distinct question in relation to consolidated financial statements is whether or not to provide a consolidation of these fund financial statements and if this should be in addition to or instead of the fund financial statements. In governments, non-profits and for-profits in which there is only a partial use of funds, the general answer is to produce one set of consolidated financial statements, perhaps with separate recognition of funds on the face of the financial statements or in the notes and perhaps also with a few fund financial statements, paralleling the case in which a group of for-profits adds a set of financial statements for the parent alone or a set of summary financial statements for a major subsidiary.

The most developed, complete use of fund accounting for organisations as a whole is in US state and local governments and this now requires, in addition to fund financial statements, one set of consolidated financial statements for each organisation as a whole – known as the government-wide financial statements. The fund financial statements reflect clear matters of external and internal control. It is much harder to identify what the government-wide financial statements reflect. Of course, they reflect the organisation as a whole – a persuasive argument for an investor or lender in a for-profit. It is much less persuasive for an investor in a government who holds bonds that are secured on the general power (sometimes termed the competence in continental Europe) of the government to tax, with added emphasis when a higher-level government is also providing implicit or explicit security. Perhaps, then, the provision of fund financial statements and government-wide financial statements is the optimal solution in practice, leaving it to the reader of the financial reports to determine which set is the most relevant and reliable.

Of the accrual accounting issues that do not generally apply in for-profit accounting, heritage assets, infrastructure assets and non-exchange transactions are three good examples. Heritage assets are land and buildings of historical importance, artifacts and artworks, often in museum collections. Sometimes referred to as public domain assets or patrimony, they are highly prized, often irreplaceable, enjoyed by all – sometimes all the world – though the government has the duty to preserve and maintain them.

Accounting requires the audited financial statements of any organisation to be comprehensive, reporting on all revenues, expenses, assets, liabilities and cash flows, not selections from them, and accounting standards define what is meant by this comprehensiveness. Accounting defines these items of the public domain as assets and therefore requires them to be included in the balance sheet and, when relevant, a related depreciation charge to be made in the operating statement. From the point of view of the whole internal control system (including many other factors than just the accounting system), governments commonly recognise the need to have registers of heritage assets and signal that need in the audited financial statements. The common controversy is whether or not the audited financial statements should record financial values.

The valuation of heritage assets is controversial in practice and theory. In practice, it can often be said to be part of the definition of heritage assets that historical costs are not available, for the obvious reason that there never was a transaction underlying them or because, if there was, it was not recorded reliably or the record is not available. Similarly, groups of heritage assets can typically be ones that are not bought and sold and, often, if they are, the market price is unique to the specific asset sold. The practical problems of determining a fair value can be prohibitive.

One theoretical issue is whether these items of the public domain are assets in any accountant's sense of assets or not. For example, it could be said that the reason for there never having been a transaction for a particular item, and no market price, is it is not an asset in that sense. For the accounting system to derive a financial value may be not only inappropriate but also could easily be offensive – for a war memorial, for example. A further issue (for assets thought appropriate to value) is the reliability of any derived value and any depreciation charge associated with it, given that future cash flows, actual or notional, may well be irrelevant.

Common accounting policies are that all heritage assets are recognised in the balance sheet, but with nominal or zero values, similarly disclosed in the notes, or not disclosed at all. These, obviously, would not require associated depreciation charges.

Infrastructure assets are assets such as water, sewage and drainage systems, roads, tunnels and bridges, lighting systems. The main point of distinguishing them from other tangible fixed assets is that identifying each asset involves identifying as one asset a physically widespread network throughout the government area (hence the term infrastructure) assets, which can have a very long life. As with other tangible fixed assets, they are generally recognised in the balance sheet and valued in financial terms. The specific issue that they raise is the treatment of depreciation.

Infrastructure assets depreciate as a result of use and, if they are treated in the same way as other depreciable assets, the book values in the balance sheet are depreciated. There is a generally accepted alternative to this, however. It can also apply in for-profit accounting and, indeed, its first significant acceptance was in the UK water industry, when it was established as a regulated industry, regulated by the government.

The alternative to depreciation can be said to be primarily an engineer's preference over the accountant's preference for depreciation. In place of the depreciation charge to the operating statement, the cost of maintaining the infrastructure asset in the year is charged. This cost can be either the actual costs incurred or an estimate of average costs to be incurred in future years to maintain the asset. The engineering argument is that these charges are more relevant to the actual management of infrastructure assets than a depreciation charge. The main accounting concern in relation to these charges is that they are reliable, generally reflected in requiring the maintenance of an infrastructure asset to be at least to its existing standard and in requiring the management system (in addition to the accounting system) actually to use the charge that is made in the operating statements in managing the asset. The UK government and US state and local government are two good examples of this alternative to depreciation accounting for infrastructure assets.

A third accrual accounting issue that does not generally apply in for-profit accounting relates to non-exchange transactions – significant examples of which are taxes and transfers from one government to another. These are transactions for which there is no equal, or approximately equal, exchange of value. Taxation is a definitive example of this. The essential accrual accounting problems of tax revenues are, first, in principle, when did the individual tax transactions occur and, second, can the accounting system reliably record the transactions at that point at reasonable cost.

Income tax provides a good illustration of these two problems. The tax revenue from a particular taxpayer occurs when the taxpayer earned the income, but the government's accounting system does not record each taxpayer's income at the point when the taxpayer earns it. Even under a system in which income tax is deducted at source from the taxpayer's salary, the records at the point of earning the salary are not the government's records. Many other forms of income tax, including of corporations, involve a significant delay between the earning of the income and the recording by the government of that income. This means that determining income cannot be done on the basis of each transaction; it can only be done periodically and with increasing degrees of approximation as the period shortens from one year to each transaction.

The two main practical possibilities are to apply the principle of when the transaction occurred but estimate the annual tax revenues statistically or set the principle aside in favour of occurrence when the taxpayer's liability is approximately settled. Both possibilities have obvious problems and a cash basis is likely to remain typical, even in otherwise accrual-based financial statements.

8.3 Policymaking

The central government of the UK and the federal government of the USA retain the right to make their own accounting policies, albeit with the help of an advisory body in the first case and through an advisory body in the second. These codified accounting policies are used directly in the financial statements. In both countries, there is no codification of the policies used in their respective budgets for the government as a whole.

The UK government's accounting policies explicitly draw on those of the independent private sector body – the International Accounting Standards Board (IASB) – making changes to those policies wherever the government chooses as the policies of the IASB have always been written for for-profit, not governments. Since the introduction of an accrual-based accounting at national level (the respective law was passed in 2000), these policies explicitly drew on business accounting in the UK, which at that time meant the policies of the Accounting Standards Board (ASB). Following the EU requirement for UK listed companies to adopt the policies of the IASB, from 2005, the central government chose to change the business accounting from which it drew its policies to the policies of the IASB. The US government's policies do not explicitly draw on business accounting.

In business accounting, before the establishment of the Financial Accounting Standards Board (FASB), the ASB and the IASB, policies were made by bodies within the accounting profession. This direct involvement of the profession still holds in the promulgation of the International Public Sector Accounting Standards. This codified set of policies is produced by the umbrella body for the world's professional accounting bodies, the International Federation of Accountants. The policies, however, were written with the aim of making as few changes as possible to the policies of the IASB (essentially by neutralising references to business), then adding topics that are only strictly relevant in government. This set of policies has no formal status in either the UK or the USA.

The only policymaking body for government that is a direct parallel of the independent private-sector policymaking bodies for for-profit (and in the USA, private non-profit) organisations is in the USA. Established in 1984, and part of the same organisation as the FASB, the Governmental Accounting Standards Board makes policies for state and local government. These policies do not substantively and explicitly draw on business accounting, though they sometimes do substantively.

8.4 Conceptual frameworks

The independent accounting standard-setting bodies all have conceptual framework projects alongside their sets of accounting standards. The projects began and are most influential in the context of standard-setting for businesses. If the Accounting Principles Board (established in the USA in 1959) can be said to be the first standard-setter that is still recognisable as such (and in a few of its pronouncements, still relevant), then its conceptual framework was the first one. All of these conceptual frameworks and their relationships with their associated accounting standards are, in essence, the same. They all attempt to improve accounting standards by establishing, as it were, a constitution of fundamental principles from which the more specific accounting standards can naturally follow or draw on. They have increasingly been seen as frameworks for the standard-setters themselves to use rather than the decisionmakers directly.

They all posit that the objective of financial statements is that they should be useful for external decisionmakers, while identifying various constraints on this usefulness. Those constraints are that their usefulness must include the reliability of the financial statements, they hypothesise a set of such decisionmakers, hypothesise a set of typical decisions made by them in relation to those financial statements and include basic definitions of elements of the financial statements. The obvious problem with these deductions is that, in principle, the decisionmakers will have different needs. The frameworks have offered no way to reconcile any expected differences, beyond positing that if the needs of investors are satisfied, then everyone else's will be, too (a position, by the way, that would be quickly unsustainable if it were to be applied to all the affairs of any given company, not just its financial statements). The other common aspects are that accounting standards only relate to material items in the financial statements and the frameworks are all conscious that the benefits of the financial statements should outweigh the costs of preparing them.

They are all statements of the policymakers about what financial statements *ought* to be. In contrast, the associated accounting standards are statements about what *is*, in the hope that the standards will be fully complied with in practice. From the beginning, this contrast has been a continual challenge. At bottom, this is because the decision-usefulness criterion that they all posit inevitably leads to the conclusion that financial statements should use *current* values, whereas the existing sets of standards to some extent or another used – and use – *historical* costs. It is very hard, some would say impossible, to identify the decision-usefulness at the balance sheet date of the historical cost of plant and equipment purchased five years before, for example. In the case of the first such conceptual framework, drawn up by the Accounting Principles Board, the challenge was too great for the Board, so the conceptual framework was abandoned in favour of the then status quo of historical cost.

Moreover, in many other cases since – involving more specific controversies in for-profit accounting – the conceptual frameworks appeared to fail to bolster the enforcement of the standard-setters' preferred accounting policies in the face of alternative policies preferred by the management of companies, with or without the support of government agencies. The inherent politicisation of accounting policymaking and the continual lack of power of the standard-setters have long raised questions about the purpose of these conceptual frameworks.

They do add to the dignity and legitimacy of the office of standardsetters, especially in that they appeal to the public interest – implicitly in opposition to the private interests of company management, but this is a tenuous judgement. Over their 50-year history, they have existed alongside a substantial increase in the adoption of current values in the financial statements, which should be a positive part of any judgement. Even this has to be qualified, however, given the more recent dominance of the concept of fair value – a concept that precisely did not emerge from the conceptual frameworks, but, instead, from its ad hoc, and contradictory, adoption in small parts of specific accounting standards over those 50 years at least. Indeed, the emerging consensus of fair value as a value determined purely by the market contradicted the academic consensus that selling prices should be net of the costs of selling, even if those costs are determined by the organisation. The adoption of fair value also remains only partial, without comprehensive conceptual explanation of which line items it should not be applied to and why.

What seems, on the face of it, strange about these conceptual frameworks is that they were increasingly developed *after* a set of accounting standards, not before. Although their purpose was to provide a constitution for individual standards, they have always necessarily had to confront pre-existing sets of standards, even if they were in the early years only practices. Each time a new body was established, a conceptual framework might have seemed the rational place to begin, but in no case could the new body have started with a clean slate of accounting standards.

Accounting standard-setters for the public sector have developed similar projects, though the significant ones have only, as yet, been in the USA. Neither the one for state and local government, nor the one for the federal government has had overtly to confront the conceptual frameworks for the private sector and, while they share many of the same basic elements, they naturally emphasise elements of government that do not apply to the private sector. They do not collapse users' needs into a dominant set of users, such as a parallel for investors, and they emphasise the importance of budgets in financial reporting, limiting any reference to budgets to those financial statements, not to the budgets themselves.

In the UK, the adoption of the standards of the IASB as the basis for government accounting at all levels might presume the adoption of the associated conceptual framework, but the immediately preceding accrual-based accounting, either at national or local level, was not underpinned by a conceptual framework. It is perhaps better to assume that there is, as yet, no such framework.

Probably the most pressing question for a conceptual framework for government accounting – for standard-setters and theorists – in determining what ought to be, is whether or not and, if so, how government accounting should be different from for-profit and non-profit accounting. In the case of International Public Sector Accounting Standards, this will presumably be answered with only marginal differences, based as they are on the for-profit standards of the IASB. The many and various governments that argue government accounting should be very different presumably have an incentive to develop a conceptual framework that might successfully counter accrual-based financial reporting.

FURTHER READING

Chow, D., Humphrey, C. and Moll, J. (2007) 'Developing whole of government accounting in the UK', *Financial Accountability and Management*, 23(1): 27–54.

Granof, M. (2010) *Government and Not-for-profit Accounting* (5th edn), Wiley.

Grossi, G., Newberry, S., Bergmann, A., Bietenhader, D., Tagesson, T., Christiaens, J., Van Cauwenberge, P. and Rommel, J. (2009) 'Whole of government accounting: international trends', *Public Money and Management*, 29(4): 209–18.

Heald, D. (2003) 'Value for money tests and accounting treatment in PFI schemes', *Accounting, Auditing and Accountability Journal*, 16(3): 342–71.

Heald, D. and Georgiou, G. (2000) 'Consolidation principles and practices for UK government sector', *Accounting and Business Research*, 30(2): 153–67.

Heald, D. and Georgiou, G. (2009) 'Whole of government accounts developments in the UK: conceptual, technical and timetable issues', *Public Money and Management*, 29(4): 219–27.

Jones, R. and Pendlebury, M. (2004) 'A theory of the published accounts of local authorities', *Financial Accountability and Management*, 20(3), August: 305–25.

Plummer, E., Hutchison, P. and Patton, T. (2007) 'GASB No. 34's Governmental Financial Reporting Model: evidence on its information relevance', *Accounting Review*, 82(1): 205–40.

Walker, R., Dean, G. and Edwards, P. (2004) 'Infrastructure reporting: attitudes of preparers and potential users', *Financial Accountability and Management*, 20(4): 351–75.

Chapter 9

Auditing

The fundamentals of auditing are common to all organisations. There are, however, distinctive aspects to government auditing: the definition of audit independence, the expanded scope of auditing to include the financial and regularity audit and performance audit, internal control and internal auditing, attitudes to materiality and budget auditing.

9.1 External auditing

Auditing is a key part of government accounting, and has been from time immemorial. In modern governments, auditors strive to provide an independent, public view of the government.

They cannot provide a completely independent view. The most fundamental reason is that auditing, by its nature, is not routinely adversarial. Auditors depend on cooperation with the auditees and, because of that alone, their independence will be compromised. In the abstract, it might be imagined that, if an independent view of government is imperative, giving auditors the power to be adversarial – to dispense with cooperation – would produce better government, but what is at stake is government itself, and governments do not hand over their sovereignty to auditors. The power that auditors are given and the levels of independence they attain are continually contested. In this, they are no different from any other group in society, but it is what they do that distinguishes them. They share a common currency with accountants – money – but what makes auditors exceptional is that they satisfy the age-old demand for an independent view of public money.

This demand is of the commonsense kind. It envisages a view of government that is not dependent on the government's own views. It also envisages a view that is not dependent on anyone else's view: it is impartial, unbiased, apolitical. The demand is for an independent view in fact and also in appearance. It expects a view that is not influenced by any personal prejudices of the auditors, whether these appear to derive from circumstances that compromise the auditors or are just auditors' attitudes of mind. It expects the view, as far as possible, to be based on evidence. It calls for an accurate, reliable, objective, non-partisan, professional view of government.

This demand is, of course, unrealistic. In some jurisdictions, it is even outweighed by the demand for government officials to be directly accountable to voters, whereby the auditors are headed by a politician whose mandate is subject to a specific popular election – a common practice in the USA. Yet, the demand is pervasive, naturally so. In continental Europe, it is typically satisfied by auditors being given judicial, or at least quasi-judicial, standing in the Courts of Auditors. It underpins the private sector professional accounting bodies. Because the demand is perennial, albeit waxing and waning in the wake of scarcity of revenues or financial scandals for example, and because it cannot be wholly satisfied, government auditing is continually striving to provide an independent view of government.

One essence of this independence is, of course, that the auditor is independent of the auditee, which is to be expected in any audit, whether in government, for-profit or non-profit organisations. In sovereign governments, however, there is a second essence of independence, which highlights its importance and its inherent difficulty.

In a sovereign government the auditee is the executive. The auditors are separate from the executive. At national levels (in countries other than those covered by the Courts of Auditors), the head is often known as the auditor general. In both the UK and the USA, the word 'comptroller' is also still used, so, in the UK, the head is the comptroller and auditor general, while in the USA he or she is the comptroller general. This term comes from medieval English, deriving from medieval French. It may reflect and bolster the dignity of the office, but it is not a word that is used in ordinary English. More importantly, its substantive meaning in this context is an anachronism. It used to mean that the head of the audit was a fundamental part of the internal financial controls (a controller) and therefore of the executive, but, in the USA, this is no longer the case and in the UK, although the comptroller function still applies, it is in a minor sense and does not compromise the head's separation from the executive. The generic terms for the auditors of national governments are the supreme auditor at the head of a supreme audit institution.

The supreme audit institutions are created by and carry out their work under the law. The legislature acts, of course, on behalf of the public. On the face of it, it makes no sense to argue that the auditors should also be independent of the legislature: auditors are auditing public money and the legislature – as the public's representative – is the sovereign power. Using the parallel of auditing for-profit organisations, the auditors are independent of management and it would make no sense to argue that the auditor should also be independent of the shareholders. Yet, the second essence of independence in a sovereign government argues just that: the auditors should be independent of the legislature.

The reason is that the legislature is political and a political position is not an independent one. If the legislature is dominated by the political party of the executive, the auditors cannot be independent of the auditee if they are dependent on the legislature. If the legislature is dominated by the main political party in opposition, the auditors can be independent of the auditee, but cannot be seen to be independent of the views of others – in this case, of the dominant political party. If the legislature is not dominated by any one party, it is the embodiment of the partial, biased, political views of others, some of which conform to those of the government, some of which do not. In all cases, the demand is for auditors to give a view of government that is above the political fray.

In lower-level governments, the context is different, but the demand is the same. Such governments do not themselves have legislatures, but the potential for inappropriate influence from the associated sovereign governments is there. The sovereign governments can also, through the law or regulations, help to bolster the independence of the auditors from their own political councils, however.

The demand for an independent view of government is satisfied by an audit that is known as an external audit, in which the main sense of being external to the government is that the auditors are not employed by the auditee but contracted (formally or informally) either by a higher-level government, government agency or the auditee itself to carry out the audit. In most sovereign governments of the world, this sense of being 'external' is difficult. In the first place, it suggests that the government has handed over some of its sovereignty – an unlikely event. In one sense or another, government auditors are not external but part of the government, even in cases where the constitution separates them from other branches of government, as it does in the US federal government, for example. In the second place, in a national government, it raises the question of how any citizen can be independent of that citizen's own government. A facetious response, unaware of the realities of auditing, would be that the government auditors should be foreigners.

The term 'external audit' is still proper, but in practical cases it encompasses different degrees of independence. External auditors, in not being employed by the auditee, are not part of the auditee's internal systems. The auditors who are part of the internal systems are internal auditors, who naturally could be employees of the auditee but could also be contracted to perform the service without violating the sense of being 'internal'. There is an important sense in which they too provide an independent view – in their case, of the internal control system. Such a view cannot have all of the independence dimensions of an external audit, but it can be usefully independent of top management, with a direct reporting line to those in charge of governance.

The continual tension between the demand for independence and the fact that independence is always compromised to some extent is resolved, formally at least, by the core definition of audit independence being based on each auditor's attitude of mind. However compromised the auditor's situation may be, the auditor is expected to have an independent attitude towards the auditee and towards other external influences. There are many aspects of the auditor's situation that can affect this attitude of mind, however. In extreme, but far from uncommon, situations in the world, government auditors' lives are at risk; in less extreme situations, their livelihoods are. Attitudes of mind can be noble and inspiring, but the architecture of audit independence requires more specific foundations. Ultimately, those foundations are stronger when auditors have direct support from the public.

The compromises embedded in government auditing include that it is:

■ part of government
■ not generally adversarial
■ paid for by government
■ often using government management of premises, equipment and supplies, as well as human resources
■ judged by the same values as government
■ subject to the same difficulties in balancing inputs, outputs and outcomes when judging performance.

Independent situations need to be extracted from these inherently dependent ones.

The audit mandate in written form, including written auditing standards, is necessary. Being able to tie this to international standards (of the International Organization of Supreme Audit Institutions or the International Federation of Accountants) adds to the legitimisation of the mandate. The national law will specify minimum reporting requirements of the audit (including the timing of the reports and the nature of the audit opinions), but independence requires that the planning, programming and conduct of the audit be the responsibility of the auditors. In the financial and regularity audits, this will typically be easier to attain than in the performance audits, which naturally are subject to more intensive political interest.

The challenges are especially striking in sovereign governments. The budget for the auditors is plainly a sensitive aspect of this, as reducing budgets is an obvious recourse for those who want to curtail audit activity and, in difficult cases, recourse to the legislature and the public beyond are the ways that auditors protect themselves. Denying access to premises, people and records is another way to compromise independence. Special difficulties lie in drawing the line between sensitive information that the auditors must have access to and the information that is too sensitive (at sovereign level, involving security) even for auditors. Removal of auditors from office is a continual threat, so conditions of auditor tenure are the response, with lengthy, fixed terms of office, perhaps to retirement age, and procedures for removal from office akin to the procedures for removal of judges. Threats to modify or suppress audit reports are continual. Allowing auditees to comment on reports before their publication is conventional and potentially compromising, so the procedures to reduce the threats take account of this.

These are rarified aspects of independence, often involving constitutions. The more quotidian relations between individual auditors and their auditees are also addressed by auditing standards. They are not intrinsically different from audits in for-profits and non-profits. Auditing standards generally call for good relations between them, but not *too* good, no responsibility of the auditee in the audit, no audit participation in the management of the auditee and no personal involvement by any of the auditors in the auditee.

In lower-level governments, there is an aspect of audit independence that is not common in for-profits and non-profits, though it has been continually debated: the appointment of auditors. In principle, audit independence is greater when the auditor's appointment is not made by the auditee itself but a government agency. For example, the auditors of local government and the local bodies of the National Health Service in England are made by a national public body. The independence that this adds depends on many things and may not be substantial if the practical effect is that a given auditor audits a given auditee for a number of years, but it is of particular interest.

9.2 Financial and regularity audits

There are two broad categories of external audits of government: financial and regularity audits, and performance audits. Both categories have parallels in external auditing of for-profit and non-profit organisations and, indeed, the financial statement audit that is part of the financial and regularity audits is common to all organisations. Both categories have distinctive features in government auditing, however.

The financial statement audit is one part of financial and regularity audits. It is the most prominent part of an audit and is the most homogeneous in definition. It is the core of the work of the professional accounting bodies. It is determined by law and governments themselves, but is often based on the pronouncements of those accounting bodies. Its method and products are defined in great detail and, with only minor changes in terminology, are applicable to for-profits, non-profits and governments internationally. This homogeneity is achieved by presenting the methods and products as purely technical, financial matters. The financial statement audit is carried out every year and relates to the annual financial statements of all reporting entities within the government.

The final product of the financial statement audit is the auditors' (or, when there is added emphasis on the opinion being of one person, the auditor's) opinion on whether or not the general-purpose financial statements fairly present what they purport to present and conform to the law related to financial statements. The opinions are published with the financial statements, clearly identifying the financial statements they relate to and, equally importantly, clearly identifying the other information that might be included with the financial statements to which the opinions do not relate. The opinions are presented in boilerplate English, with variations according to jurisdiction. Fair presentation can be expressed as 'presents fairly', 'true and fair view' and 'properly presents' in specific contexts. Fair presentation is typically now expressed as – even limited to – being in accordance with a specific set of published accounting policies.

The financial statement audit can only produce opinions, not matters of fact. The audit is always dependent on the internal controls of the government, whether or not the auditor chooses to depend on them to a lesser degree. These opinions refer to two different sets of accounting information. First, are matters of fact – the bookkeeping records of transactions, reconciled to bank statements. Second, are themselves opinions – the annual aggregation, measurement and valuation of revenues, expenses, assets, liabilities and cash flows (or different terms, depending on the accounting basis adopted). Under any accounting basis, the auditors' opinion significantly relates to the records of transactions. The extent to which the opinion extends beyond those records of transactions depends on the basis of accounting. Under an accrual basis of accounting, the auditors' opinion extends much further than under a pure cash basis of accounting because the amount and importance of measurement and valuation opinions are greater.

The financial statement audit has been an essential part of government audit for at least a generation, but another part of the financial and regularity audits is much older. This focuses on the records of transactions and on the transactions themselves, asking were they proper? The propriety of spending and collection of income, the safeguarding of assets and the appropriateness of liabilities, as well as the accuracy and completeness of the records, are judged in the context of public money. The term 'probity' elevates this 'appropriateness' to the 'integrity' of those records of transactions. Propriety and probity mean the records of transactions have been found to be free of error and not fraudulent, and the transactions themselves have been neither wasteful nor extravagant.

Propriety and probity are relevant to for-profits. They can be imposed on them by law, such as by a host country proscribing what it defines as corruption in the for-profit's dealings in foreign countries. In for-profits, however, they are much more commonly subsumed within an overall objective of being profitable. In governments (and non-profits, of course), propriety and probity have to be explicit and are much harder to subsume on any grounds. The law will be explicit about the propriety and probity expected within governments, and the auditors' role will be to give an opinion on whether or not the transactions conformed to that law.

In addition to the long-standing tradition of auditing propriety and probity, the financial and regularity audits of government also include the long-standing practice in modern governments of auditing whether the transactions conformed to the budget or not. In many governments, the budget, too, will be authorised by law, and the audit will similarly provide an opinion on whether or not the transactions conform to that aspect of the law.

These core parts of the financial and regularity audits are carried out every year and relate to the general purpose annual financial statements of all reporting entities within each government. There are many other services provided by auditors that relate to financial and regularity matters, which may be ad hoc, relate to only parts of financial statements, parts of the reporting entities or parts of government. Some of these are called audits, but different terms are sometimes used to emphasise that, while they are carried out by auditors, the auditors are providing lower levels of assurance than those provided by the core financial and regularity audits. The terminological precision is clearest in the USA, where professional standards use the term 'attestation' to refer to lower levels of assurance than would occur for an 'audit'. Also, within attestation standards, 'review of financial statements' is used to refer to such lower levels than 'compilation of financial statements'. In governments, some specific examples of these other financial and regularity services commonly provided by auditors are certifying grant claims from higher-level governments, reporting only on internal control systems (rather than as part of the financial statement audit), reporting only on compliance with laws and regulations (rather than as part of the financial statement audit) and reporting on budgets.

All parts of the financial and regularity audits overlap with judgements about the performance of government. It is not possible to give an opinion on accrual-based financial statements without giving an opinion on the going concern status of the government, which is strictly a matter of performance. Neither is it possibly, strictly, to give an opinion about propriety or probity without giving an opinion about outputs and outcomes. The law might attempt to reduce the financial and regularity audits to a set of written criteria, which would obviate the need for wider opinions of the auditors, but it will not be wholly successful in reducing the everchanging complexities of government rules. Performance audits, which address economy, efficiency and effectiveness directly, are required.

9.3 Performance audits

The second broad category of external audits of government relates to the audit of outputs and outcomes, which are performance audits (also known as economy, efficiency and effectiveness audits or value for money audits). Such audits are common in for-profit and non-profit organisations, but as consulting exercises carried out spasmodically at the behest of the organisations themselves. In governments, however, performance audits of each governmental organisation are required continually. They cannot be carried out continually on all aspects of government, though, so parts of government are subject to performance audit each year. The decision as to what to audit when is the auditor's to make, not the executive's or the legislature's. There will, however, commonly be situations in which public controversy about a government activity will be so strong that the auditor will have, in effect, no choice but to carry out the performance audit of a particular aspect of government giving rise to the controversy. Audit reports on performance do not have a standard form – they are made to the legislature or those otherwise charged with governance, but the auditee is typically given at least the opportunity to comment on a report before it is published.

Performance audits are very politically sensitive. Financial and regularity audits can be, too, but routinely are not as they have largely been reduced to technical, financial matters. Performance audits must be audits of financial matters (as performance must include costs if it is to have economic meaning), but they must also be audits of non-financial outputs and outcomes. They must, in the end, question government policies, too. The demand for performance audits is a demand for an independent view of the performance of government – the economy, efficiency and effectiveness of the policies and their implementation. This demand cannot ultimately be satisfied in anything other than political terms and the performance auditor is inevitably part of the political fray – even though the demand is for the auditor to be above it.

In governments in which it is politically unacceptable for auditors to question their policies (which is probably in most of the world), the methodology of performance audits addresses this contradiction by taking the government's policies as given (not overtly questioning those policies) and then judging the economy, efficiency and effectiveness of the implementation of those policies. Moreover, in such governments, the performance audit mandate can limit the auditors' judgements to whether the governmental organisations themselves have good control systems that explicitly include the determination, implementation and monitoring of policies, thereby obviating the need for auditors to impart their own judgements on the governments' performance.

The imperative of an independent audit is at least to be accurate, based on evidence, reliable and, therefore, objective. In financial and regularity audits, by the nature of their focus, this is more naturally achievable. The ultimate focus of a performance audit, however, is a matter of political opinion and, therefore, objectivity is much harder, in principle, to achieve. In practice, though, it is often achieved in each particular audit by focusing on the narrower, more measurable, more technical matters of performance, thereby avoiding the wider, more qualitative, more political questions. In the complex rough-and-tumble of government, there is never a shortage of such matters to address, in procurement practices, duplication of effort by employees and other work that has little purpose, idleness, overstaffing, inefficient stores, corruption and so on. Similarly, performance audits can address systems, such as the accounting system, focusing on technical matters such as the definition of relevant costs and the timeliness of reporting. All of these matters can, ultimately, attract political support, but, taken separately, the apparent weaknesses that performance audit reports typically identify are useful.

When the performance audits embrace wider questions of performance, professional accounting and auditing skills have to be supplemented by other professional skills. The common sense of the auditor would complement, but not be a substitute for, a soldier's understanding or a teacher's, an engineeer's, a human resource manager's or a marketer's understanding. Having a mix of skills in the performance audit team does not necessarily produce a satisfactory response to the challenge of the interdisciplinary understanding of performance, though – that depends on the work of the team. That said, the fact that the team is interdisciplinary should provide more of a joined-up view of government to counter an entrenched factional, organisational views of performance.

In the absence of absolute measures of success, performance audits make the best of what is available. Benchmarking is the norm and comparisons are ubiquitous. These comparisons are made over time (with previous periods' performance), through space (with comparable organisational units or programmes within the government, with comparable units or programmes beyond, including in the private sector) and with predetermined standards generated in the same way. They are necessary, but the conclusions about performance are never fixed, never certain, always contestable.

The performance audits of each governmental organisation can provide the basis for reports on performance that cut across them. The comparisons of performance inherent in the audits invite such treatment. The reports are most useful when there are many relatively homogeneous organisations to compare, as in local governments and other local authorities within a jurisdiction. They will not be produced by the performance auditors themselves, at least not in that capacity, but by a regulatory agency or higher-level government body. They can have the advantage over performance audits, depending on the resources applied to them, that the comparisons can be more wide-ranging, providing a bigger population to observe. The results of such reports often take the form of pointing out how much the lowest-performing organisations could improve if they performed as well as the highest-performing ones. The essence of a given report of this kind might not seem different from a performance audit report on an organisation by that organisation's auditor, particularly in that comparisons with others are common to both, but in principle they are different. A performance audit report depends on information from one organisation, reported on at one point, supplemented by comparisons, while reports on performance that depend on comparisons are statistical reports. The relevance and reliability of the two kinds of reports must be judged differently.

9.4 Internal control

Financial and regularity audits, as well as performance audits, depend on the auditee's system of internal control. They make risk-based assessments about the strength of the system and, in the light of those assessments, judge how much additional audit work needs to be done. When the auditors judge that the internal controls are strong, their opinions will rely on them more; when they are weak, less.

The systems of internal control, in principle, cover everything that the organisation does – the planning, execution and monitoring of all its activities. The systems can only deal with those factors that are within the organisation's control. Parties external to the organisation may provide useful information about that internal control and contribute to achieving the organisation's objectives, but the internal control is central. In its widest sense, it is the management control of the government. It is expected to be delineated in written form, with as much output measurement as is compatible with better management.

The traditional focus of internal control systems – namely the accounting system – and financial and regularity audits have been the same:

- safeguarding financial resources against loss due to waste, abuse, mismanagement, errors, fraud and other irregularities
- adhering to laws, regulations and management directives about financial resources
- having accurate records of transactions
- producing relevant and reliable financial reports in a timely fashion, including general purpose audited financial statements, fairly presented.

The dominance of money and money measurement in all of these matters makes these aspects of the internal control systems naturally suited to formal, written control.

The kinds of long-standing detective and preventative controls include:

- authorisation procedures for ordering and receiving goods and services and processing payments, making payments and claiming refunds related thereto
- authorisation procedures for disposing of assets
- the segregation of duties between those who authorise, process, record and review financial transactions, and the appropriate supervision of all
- controls over access to financial resources, including processes for collecting and paying in money
- controls over financial records
- systematic verifications of financial balances
- systematic financial reconciliations, including bank reconciliations
- systematic financial reporting and, with added emphasis in the context of accrual-based external financial reporting, systems for ensuring compliant and fair presentations.

In recent decades, these narrower senses of internal control, based on the accounting system, have been extended to include all aspect of management control, whether in for-profits, non-profits or governments.

A significant impetus for this came from the business scandals at the turn of the century. In principle and in practice it is common to define 'internal control' as descending from the top management's philosophy and style, through the organisational structure (by assigning authority and responsibility within it, including how authority and responsibility are delegated and appropriate lines of reporting on all aspects of management) and including the human resource policies and practices. Such a view of internal control in government naturally includes the output measures and outcomes that are the ultimate focus of the performance audit.

External auditors are not the only ones with explicit responsibilities for the internal control system. Internal auditors also provide a view, independent of top management, with a direct reporting line to those in charge of governance, perhaps through an audit and assurance committee. The internal auditors and those charged with governance also take a risk management approach to internal controls, in reporting to the management board on potential risks and risk management in the government organisation.

However strong these internal control systems may be, and in any one government may have been, they can never be wholly relied on. People make mistakes, they can circumvent controls by colluding with two or more people, within the government and without, and management can override the written controls. Moreover, there is a fundamental tension in the design of any internal control system between more control and better services. Organisations do not exist to be controlled; they exist to provide services. Control is necessary for organisations to exist but it is not sufficient and what is the necessary amount and kind of control is always going to be difficult to determine.

A recurring problem for internal control of public money is that there is often less tolerance of any trade-off between control and better services. Travel and hospitality expenses of public servants, and their salaries, tend to have to be subject to the kinds of strict controls that would not be envisaged in for-profit organisations, whatever effects the controls may have on the services they provide. Having official credit cards to pay for official lunches may be prevalent in both for-profits and governments, but it will not take much of a financial scandal for them to be withdrawn in governments.

The internal control systems themselves are designed, therefore, not to provide *absolute* assurance but *reasonable* assurance that the government is achieving its objectives, whether the systems' objectives are narrowly or widely drawn. In addition, the auditors make risk-based assessments of the internal controls, in that they do not check every detail. Their assessments of internal control also, therefore, do not provide absolute but only reasonable assurance.

The widening of internal control systems from the narrower financial control of the accounting system to include everything in the management control of a government, and the concomitant pervasiveness of output measurement, begs a fundamental question for all of us: can information systems be as reliable in generating and storing non-financial numbers as they can with financial numbers?

The myriad verifications of financial balances and the ultimate bank reconciliations inherent in accounting systems cannot be fully replicated for non-financial numbers. This suggests that auditing non-financial numbers will require more testing of the numbers themselves (in addition to the control systems for those numbers) than is necessary for financial ones, though whether or not the implications of this are generally understood by those advocating the ever-increasing use of non-financial performance measures is perhaps unclear.

9.5 Materiality

The government's records of transactions – on which all the accounting and auditing is based – are required to be comprehensive. Equally, the financial reports drawn from them and (in reporting on internal controls) related to them and the associated audit opinions are abstractions that have, at their base, a challenge: how to extract relevant and reliable meaning from the complex detail. The information revolution continues to promise better solutions, by providing external users with direct access to the records, but old ways persist. Use of the concept of 'materiality' is an important example of this.

'Materiality' emerged in accounting and auditing to provide a more specific name for the use of the accountant's or auditor's professional judgement in deciding on what was significant in the reports. The financial reports are based on comprehensive records, defined in relation to the particular report – that is, the general purpose financial statements must include all records of the organisation, though the comprehensiveness of special-purpose reports is often defined more narrowly. The reports, however, only detail what is judged material, the applicable accounting standards are only applied to material items, the assurance on internal controls only relates to material items, including the audit opinion thereon, and the audit's opinions about compliance and fairness of presentation are only concerned with material respects.

The explicit appeal to professional judgement about materiality naturally emerged as the work of accountants and auditors became more controversial during the second half of the twentieth century and the subsequent accounting and auditing standards emerged. In the early stages of this process, materiality was otherwise indefinable: it precisely meant that what was significant was a pure matter of judgement. In most cases, in both the government and the private sector, it remains a matter of judgement, which regulators and other standardsetters are coy about defining any more specifically, notwithstanding the obvious tide of principle and practice that demands an objective reference for these judgements. The coyness is understandable, if only because the publication of a definition facilitates the fraudulent in covering up their frauds, by providing a 'bright line' in financial terms (say, transactions of £1000 or more) below which there will be no substantive testing. Quantitative measures of materiality are set, but they are hedged by reference to qualitative assessments.

Typical quantitative measures of materiality are naturally drawn from the fundamental aggregates in the financial statements, of revenues, expenses, assets, liabilities and cash flows (or different terms that reflect different accounting bases). Material items of revenues and expenses might then be defined to include any item that is more than X per cent of gross expenses and material assets as any asset that is more than X per cent of gross assets. Multiple measures might be used in different parts of the government, especially where special-purpose financial statements or audit opinions are concerned.

These quantitative financial measures are hedged in two ways. First, they are accompanied by nuance, which emphasises that the measures can be misleading. When a large proportion of a balance sheet's assets is made up of valuations of infrastructure assets, for example, in most cases it would not be useful in auditing the safeguarding of assets to define materiality as a percentage of total assets as infrastructure assets are much less likely to be misappropriated. Second, they are accompanied by qualifications, which emphasise that, in dealing with public money, there are sensitivities not necessarily reflected in monetary amounts. The salaries and travel and hospitality expenses of public servants again seem to have to be judged against stricter standards than is the case in the private sector, so with much added emphasis, an audit of the government auditors would do well to have a low threshold for defining materiality of their expenses.

The guidance on materiality is small relative to its importance. Most of it relates to general purpose financial reporting. In other contexts, it is even less and sometimes non-existent. One obvious example of the latter is in performance audits, where the weighting towards non-financial matters reduces the relevance of quantitative financial measures and quantitative guidance about non-financial measures would be much more various, probably restrictively so, because of the specificity of the measures. Another example is in popular reporting, which again, by its nature, involves much greater levels of abstraction from the underlying records of transactions. In such cases, materiality would have to strike the very difficult balance between the relevance of information to non-expert audiences and a trivialisation of the underlying complexities.

Materiality is, even by the standards of most government accounting and auditing issues, an esoteric matter, so is left to accountants and auditors to define it. It is a good example, though, of an accounting and auditing concept that has very significant effects on accounting and auditing and, as such, is one that is open to being contested. Typical normative questions follow, such as, as financial reports are directed at external users, should not those external users define materiality? More narrowly, as, in government, those external users are primarily legislatures or other councils of politicians, should not those politicians define materiality?

In practice, the accountants' and auditors' definitions of materiality are qualitatively judged by those external users in retrospect, in the aftermath of a material financial scandal.

9.6 Budget auditing

Budgeting is a core part of the rational planning, execution and monitoring cycle. Full accountability would require that all stages in the budgetary cycle be publicly transparent. As none would doubt that an audit is indispensable in this and all financial reporting of actuals is audited, it would also require all other stages to be subject to an audit in some form.

There are two reasons for adding emphasis to this rational argument. The first is that the interests of politicians and the public in this cycle are overwhelmingly weighted towards the budget – the point of the cycle that is of most relevance externally, but the least reliable. The second is that the annual cycle of incremental budgets can easily proceed from original budget to original budget, even with a revised budget, unanchored by any explicit comparison with actual results. In the absence of an audit, the scope for biasing budgets – either in requesting too much or too little or simply getting them wrong – is high.

One obvious objection to these arguments is that an audit of budgets can never provide the same levels of assurance as an audit of financial statements of actuals. Financial statements are similarly dependent on matters of opinion, but their foundation is verifiable records of transactions, a foundation that budgets do not share. The commonplace response to this objection is to define the lower levels of assurance to be provided by a budget audit, making any concomitant changes in terminology from 'audit' to 'assurance'.

The two elements of budgets – as targets and predictions – are addressed differently, but, in each case, the overall approach is the same: to evaluate internal control over the budgets, evaluate the assumptions of the budget, evaluate compliance with rules and guidelines and issue a report.

Budget audits are carried out in a number of contexts (including, in the private sector, in the context of initial public offerings), but their absence in the systematic annual financial and regularity audits remains the most fundamental weakness of rational control in practice.

FURTHER READING

Bourn, J. (2007) *Public Sector Auditing*, Wiley.

Clark, C., De Martinis, M. and Krambia-Kapardis, M. (2007) 'Audit quality attributes of European Union supreme audit institutions', *European Business Review*, 19(1), 40–71.

Flesher, D. and Zarzeski, M. (2002) 'The roots of operational (vfm) auditing in English-speaking nations', *Accounting and Business Research*, 32(2): 93–104, with a response by W. Funnell (2004), 34(3), 215–22.

Gendron, Y., Cooper, D. and Townley, B. (2007) 'The construction of auditing expertise in measuring government performance', *Accounting, Organizations and Society*, 32: 101–29.

Ijiri, Y. (1968) 'On budgeting principles and budget-auditing standards', *Accounting Review*, XLIII(4), October: 662–7.

Mayper, A., Granof, M. and Giroux, G. (1991) 'An analysis of municipal budget variances', *Accounting, Auditing and Accountability Journal*, 4(1): 29–50.

Miller, P., Kurunmäki, L. and O'Leary, T. (2008) 'Accounting, hybrids and the management of risk', *Accounting, Organizations and Society*, 33: 942–67.

Pendlebury, M. and Jones, R. (1983) 'Budget auditing in governmental organisations financed by taxation', *Journal of Business Finance and Accounting*, 10(4): 585–93.

Power, M. (1997) *The Audit Society*, Oxford University Press.

Skærbæk, P. (2009) 'Public sector auditor identities in making efficiency auditable: the National Audit Office of Denmark as independent auditor and modernizer', *Accounting, Organizations and Society*, 34(8): 971–87.

White, F. and Hollingsworth, K. (1999) *Audit, Accountability and Government*, Clarendon.

Index